Future You

Essential Future Technologies You Need to Know
to Survive the Digital Era

By Jason Strong

Copyright

Table of Contents

1. Introduction

It is hard to believe the World Wide Web has been in existence since just 1990. In the same 28 years it takes the average person to finally purchase their first house, the World Wide Web has morphed into a ubiquitous presence on which the whole of modern civilisation has become entirely dependant upon. With the rate of change in technology growing exponentially, it becomes both difficult and intimidating to imagine life in a further 28 years. Will fossil fuels and the resulting environmental damage destroy our world beyond repair? Will artificial intelligence become so advanced that it displaces humans as the dominant life form on earth? Who will be the winners and losers in an era of constant and rapid technological evolution? More importantly, where do you, as a blue collar, white collar, business owner or student, stand in a world where technology is transforming whole industries by the month. For some there will be boundless opportunities, for others there is only hardship and misery. The only certainty is the very reasoning for writing this book; those who are willing to learn, adapt and evolve will open themselves to immeasurable opportunity. Those who do not will find themselves quickly displaced by increasingly more capable technology.

The modern world is now entering a fourth industrial revolution. The previous three (steam, mass production, and the digital revolution) saw employment rise in line with productivity, benefiting both businesses and consumers. Higher productivity creates higher paying jobs, in turn creating more disposable income. More disposable income allows consumers to purchase more, which further increases demand and the cycle of prosperity continues. This pattern has been the catalyst for the rapid economic growth seen in developed countries for the last century or so. This fourth revolution, one where the lines between the real and digital worlds are blurring, is worryingly different, however. Employment and productivity are now diverging. Despite employment reaching a record high in much of the developed world, productivity (global output) is flat lining. The importance of this finding can not be overstated; productivity, and hence the prosperity of society, is becoming less dependent on human input. Businesses are now turning to robotics and artificial intelligence, which can be much more efficient, to fill this productivity gap. The robot revolution is spreading beyond blue collar jobs such as supermarket cashiers and restaurant waiters into white collar territory, such as lawyers, financial analysts, and even doctors. No one can assume they are safe. Are you going to simply stand by and let luck determine your fate? Or are you going to exploit and leverage the upcoming technologies and trends outlined in this book to take control of your own destiny?

Having had an extensive career in the automotive and construction industries, I have seen first-hand both the innovation and damage automation can reap. GPS led construction plant like excavators and dumpers, are now more accurate and more efficient than even the best human operators. Automated robotics can build cars quicker, cheaper and to a better quality than a human ever could. It is first-hand knowledge and experience that I bring to you, with the hope that you will embrace not only the entailed knowledge but also the corresponding advice and insights to ensure you do not get lost in the world of rapid change, but instead use it to leverage results and get ahead of your competition.

This book will give a comprehensive overview of some of the most disruptive technologies and industries in the near future, with particular focus on artificial intelligence and automation and the effects they will have on business and employment. We won't get stuck into nitty-gritty details, that is the job of other, more specialized, books. Instead, you will build a strong foundation of knowledge of how some of the most disruptive industries will change how we live and work along with the many opportunities it will create. You will learn of trends and patterns these technologies create and come to some enlightening conclusions. I'll let you into one of the biggest: you will never win a fight against technology. As technology becomes increasingly faster, cheaper and more capable, those who resist and fight will only prolong the inevitable pain and misery while those who accept it and use it to their advantage will enjoy a rewarding and prosperous life.

This book is inspired by the mantra of one of the most revered businessman of the past century, Warren Buffett. Seen as one of the most successful investors ever, he maintains that the best investment you can make is in yourself. The best place to start is by learning as much as you can, such as with this book. You are also never too old to learn or retrain; as we will see, those who are taking online degrees are on average in their mid-30s, have at least one child and are in full employment. There is no excuse. There is also no excuse to delay. As AI in the workplace gets exponentially more common, those who are the least prepared will be the first to go. Can you afford to be that person? I know I can't, so without further ado, let's address the elephant in the room and our first topic - artificial intelligence.

2. **Artificial Intelligence**

Artificial intelligence (AI) has been the buzzword in the tech world for the past few years now, with seemingly small, unproven and unprofitable businesses being snapped up for extortionate sums by the key players in the technology sector. An acute lack of AI talent in a field vital to future economic growth has created a whirlwind of acquisitions. Leading the charge, unsurprisingly, is Google, followed by the likes of Apple, Microsoft, Amazon, and Intel. Between 2013 to 2017, there was a fivefold increase in the number of AI acquisitions from 22 to 115. Other industries whose business does not rely on such technology are also jumping on the bandwagon, with Ford investing \$1 billion in Argo AI in 2017. If I could go back a few years and realign my career path, a software developer in the AI field would be a very comfortable place to be right now.

Despite being an intangible force, AI is already deeply embedded into society, perhaps irreversibly so. Even the dreaded morning commute relies on AI to make our trip safer, from anti-lock brakes in modern vehicles to smart all-wheel drive (AWD) systems ensuring wheels point firmly in the same direction as that intended. Without them, many lives would be lost each year.

Capabilities generally covered under the category of artificial intelligence include a successful understanding of human speech (think Siri and Alexa), competing in high-level strategic games (Chess and Go), military simulations, autonomous cars and interpreting complex content such as face recognition, now available on most smartphones.

These are all examples of a narrow or weak AI; artificial intelligence which has a specific intended purpose and can only do that one programmed primary task (despite doing it very well). They are weak by name but not by nature; they form very powerful and useful tools when used for the right purposes and have proved to be hugely valuable for those who utilise them. Current technology limits developers to mostly weak forms of AI but many companies are now setting their sights on general intelligence AI. Thanks to advances in computer power, processing, and storage, developers are now able to build upon weak AI, creating what is termed "strong" AI systems which would be able to draw upon its own pools of resources to solve problems long thought to be only possible by human intelligence. They would also be highly versatile and, as opposed to weak AI whose programming needs to be tailored for each and every situation, it would be able to complete a wide variety of tasks without human interference or reprogramming. It could be comparable to human intelligence insofar as its ability to identify unfamiliar problems, predict outcomes and devise unique solutions. General intelligence is where AI starts to raise concerns for some; a machine with the ability to think for itself and obtain self-awareness exposes humanity to many uncomfortable positions.

Although research into artificial intelligence first started around the 1950's, it soon became apparent that any significant progress in the field would be very difficult and a long way off. This lack of progress soon crippled future funding and innovation, resulting in long hiatus' of on and off research known as AI winters. The recent surge in funding and progress is the result of faster computation, access to masses of data (smartphones are a company's dream for obtaining data) and software developments such as machine learning and artificial neural networks (ANN), all combining to pave the way for innovation.

Although cynics are aplenty, AI is here to stay and it will only continue to further saturate into personal lives and workplaces. The stakes are high; there is much to lose if uncontrolled but much to gain if implemented responsibly. The safest way forward is to embrace change whilst ensuring full control is maintained. It is anyone's guess what a machine with the ability to think for itself would make of the world and the imminent irreparable damage humanity has unleashed on the delicate environment would take some explaining. Whether the most intelligent of computer systems will ever truly even be able to think like a human is subject to much debate, but I urge those sceptics who dismiss any possibility of a machine obtaining self-awareness and consciousness to read on with an open mind.

Machine Learning

Live and Learn

Machine learning might sound like a paradox in terms but there is certainly some credibility in the term. It is a subset of general or "strong" artificial intelligence which uses complex mathematical statistical techniques to enable computers to "learn". Although many accept a computer's apparent ability to mimic learning seemingly on its own accord merely from the input of data, many argue that this is just clever maths and is in no way comparable to a human's ability to truly learn. This claim, however, infers that full anatomical knowledge of the human brain, and how it works and learns, is known. In reality, the magnificently complex series of trillions of neurons and synapses is, at this point in time, just as much of a mystery as the origins of the universe. Without knowing fully how the brain learns it is not fair to say what else also can and cannot learn.

Machine learning systems are able to use data to come up with its own solutions and conclusions without being explicitly programmed to do so, as with weak AI. Improvements in machine learning systems, therefore, rely on the study and construction of clever software and algorithms from which a computer can learn and make predictions without interference from a human programmer. Machine learning is heavily related to computational statistics and data analytics where the computer can model a wide variety of scenarios from input data to learn what works and what doesn't to create the most likely statistical models. The quality of the output is therefore dependent on the quality of the input data and the how accurately the algorithm has been coded.

There are various tiers of machine learning, the uses of which depend on the quantity, quality, and type of input data. Supervised systems present the computer with known examples of input data as well as known desired outputs. The goal for supervised systems is to learn the general rule which maps inputs to outputs in the most efficient manner possible. Unsupervised systems, on the other hand, provide no labels to the input data and the algorithm is left to find its own structure to come up with outputs. It is, therefore, more associated with true artificial intelligence. Supervised systems provide more accurate correlations if both input and output data is known, but where data is unknown, unsupervised systems can provide acceptable results when the input sample data is large and of a decent quality.

The objective inherent to all types of systems, however, is to generalize from experience. The magnitude of success depends on the ability of a learning machine to make accurate predictions based on new, unseen input data having already drawn its own system of rules from previous data.

Facebook's news feed is perhaps the most ubiquitous use of machine learning today. Each member's news feed is personally tailored to the individual based on data from the user, such as what type of posts were looked at most and which ones were liked. The more the user interacts the more information is gathered and, assuming the algorithms are well coded, the more appropriate the content for the user. This is also the same technique advertisers' use. When browsing the internet for shoes, for example, Google will remember your searches. You may have noticed that your past searches, such as for shoes or clothing, appear in adverts in future searches. Google's algorithms learn of your search categories to try and sell you related projects in your future searches. So when you see someone presented with an advert for Viagra, it should be pretty obvious what their previous searches were!

Machine learning largely mimics the biological neural networks used for millions of years in animal brains. Artificial neural networks (ANN) are complex weaves of interconnected nodes where information can be analysed and passed around. These nodes are merely computational mechanisms where information can be received from its input; a node will then perform its pre-programmed computation and then passes the modified data onto the next node, starting the cycle again. The end of the network is formed from output nodes which compare the computed data from all previous nodes with the known answer the programmer has given it. The clever part of the neural network is its ability to use the error difference between output values passed on from previous nodes to the known output entered by the programmer and pass this error back into the network for another attempt. Knowing the error, the network can try again with different calculations to try and get closer to the desired output. It does this by weighing the connections between the nodes. Each node may have many connections into it and after every iteration, the network can increase or decrease the weighting (i.e. the influence of connection in getting closer to the desired output) of each connection in an attempt to close the error gap. It is a dynamic system of educated guesswork, using the outputs from the previous iteration to close the error gap and more closely match the calculated output to the desired output, resulting in successful "learning".

Whether this is considered true learning depends on one's definition of learning. Personally, the way in which learning is achieved matters little if the result is the same. So the question is not whether machines can learn but rather if a machine achieves the same results from learning as can their human counterparts. To attempt to answer this, however, we need to delve a little deeper into what it actually is to be human.

Hard problem of consciousness

Hard-Core

Arthur C. Clarke once wrote in his 1982 novel 2010: Odyssey Two, "Whether we are based on carbon or on silicon makes no fundamental difference; we should each be treated with appropriate respect". Many think it laughable that human traits such as consciousness and respect should even be considered applicable to AI. Whether intelligent or not machines are just a series of 1's and 0's blindly following lines of code. They cannot "feel" love as animals do, or "feel" that sense of tremendous excitement and passion when their favourite baseball team wins the World Series. Looking deeper, however, this may not be such a silly thought.

When trying to ascertain whether general intelligence can ever reach the same level of intelligence and consciousness as that of (most) humans, some deep and fundamental philosophical questions arise. Is artificial intelligence even possible? Can a synthetic machine solve problems that require intelligence as humans do? Are there limits to what machines can accomplish?

If machines are to become intelligent will they be dangerous or have the intention of causing harm? Can we ensure that machines abide by the ethics and morals coded into them? Can a machine be considered to have a mind, thoughts or conscious experiences as humans do? If so are they sentient and therefore deserve rights? That is a lot of very open and vague questions that are (certainly at this moment in time) impossible to answer and very difficult to even attempt to. The difficulty lies in the fact that we have very little knowledge and understanding of how our brain works and why we seem to have qualia (individual instances of subjective, conscious experiences such as pain, feeling regret or boredom). The magnitude of the gap in knowledge we have of the brain is colossal; the brain has an estimated 86 billion neurons, each with over 1000 connections resulting in near 100 trillion nerve connections (synapses). That's an unfathomably large number; it is at least 1000 times the number of stars in our galaxy. Recent studies of the brain estimate its storage capacity of 1 petabyte (1 million gigabytes or the equivalent of 1000 computers today). This goes some way to represent the size of the hill needed to be climbed to piece together how it all works let alone how to physically replicate it.

Perhaps asking the question of whether AI will ever be able to obtain human levels of intelligence and consciousness is the wrong question to ask. A more significant one might be whether consciousness even exists. Consciousness has long thought to be an inherently human trait which is non-physical i.e. you can't open the brain and find the stuff. Finding the link between physical brain processes and the subjective qualia we have is a deeply controversial topic known as the hard problem of consciousness, first coined by the philosopher David Chalmers in 1995. Why is there a subjective component to experience? Why do we daydream and see such deep and vivid images? Why aren't we what Chalmers coined "philosophical zombies", merely interpreting data like a computer. We don't need to think about human activities such as breathing and digesting, for these we are on autopilot, just like a zombie. Why are we not on autopilot for the rest? Chalmers argues that these experiences cannot be explained with physical means but are a fundamental component of the universe. If, for example, your parents would have unfortunately passed away before given birth to you, and you were therefore not in existence, would your conscious still manifest in some way, in some other being? Or would there just be nothing? If this line of thinking is correct, this would mean that a man-made machine would never be able to obtain the level of consciousness in humans and would therefore never truly be able to think and have experiences like humans do. If consciousness is immaterial then physics, as we know it today, would break down. Then again, this is not so different from being unable to physically explain what happened before the big bang.

For those who prefer their theories within the laws of physics, the American philosopher Daniel Dennett provides a solution for this problem of consciousness; it is an illusion. He argues that consciousness as we know it is purely the result of physical processes which can be broken down into physical fundamentals such as atoms, electrons, gravity and most likely a myriad of yet unknown quantities. This line of thought means that the brain is merely a very specialized and sophisticated information processing system and that all functions, from blinking, breathing and dreaming are merely computations resulting from networks of electrical impulses and neurons, nothing more and nothing less. To those dualists who argue that the mind must be non-physical, if we cannot explain it through science; compare it to more unenlightened times when the earth (quite logically) seemed flat and the sun appeared as if it must orbit the earth. Only once we developed the tools and technology to observe and analyse these objects could we prove that what was once deemed common sense was indeed wrong. Dennett puts forth two ways of seeing the world, one through a manifest image (clear or obvious to the mind or eye) and the other a scientific image (what is happening on a physical level with molecules, atoms etc.) To best illustrate this, think of how simple it is to swipe your finger across your phone when playing for a new high score in Candy Crush. Such a seemingly simple move for your brain is actually masking a mind-bogglingly complicated series of computations and coding behind your screen. The actual coding and physics behind the swiping action is the scientific image; it can be broken down to physical fundamentals such as electrons and atoms. Imagine teleporting a 45-year-old Isaac Newton from the prime of his life in 1687, having just written his masterpiece outlining his discovery of gravity, to the present day and presenting him with any old smartphone we take as a near basic essential today. Despite being one the most intelligent beings to grace the planet, he would be at a complete loss explaining how the pictures he is seeing on the tiny screen are moving. Being just a few millimetres thick, he may logically conclude that there cannot possibly be anything inside, so it must be some sort of non-physical explanation. This is the manifest image at play; a result of our brain being finely tuned to display only what is needed in order for us to carry out our lives in the most efficient manner. Despite being biologically very complicated, human reproduction is the most basic of human instincts and almost every woman is able to easily reproduce without needing an idea of how it actually works. This is competence without comprehension, i.e. we don't need to know how things work in order to be able to do them. Further to this, all the comprehension we currently have in the world is the result of many instances of uncomprehending competences compounding over time into ever more competent and hence comprehending systems.

I know the past few pages may have seemed as if we have deviated from AI as the subject matter, but I hope you have managed to keep up with this somewhat controversial and philosophical chapter because it all leads to one very important conclusion regarding the future of AI. By believing in materialism and the scientific image (the belief that nothing exists except matter and its movements), the brain and everything associated with it (the concept of consciousness for example) can be broken down into computations involving neurons and electron flows. There is no scientific reason therefore that we cannot replicate this system of computations, confirming that, in theory, it is indeed possible for machines to fully replicate human intelligence to a point where there is absolutely no difference between man and machine at a physical level. If this is the case, there is nothing to limit how intelligent these machines can be. Human intelligence is limited chiefly by the pace of natural evolution and the ability of the brain to fit down the birth canal. A machines "brain", however, can be as large as physics allows, creating the possibility for a more intelligent system.

It is important, however, to realise just how far away we are from this point, the computing power and tools needed to achieve this level of intelligence and replicate trillions of neural pathways is frighteningly large and it may be so impracticable to achieve that it may never happen. But I believe it is technically possible. Ironically, perhaps the only way to obtain full comprehension of the workings of the brain is by utilising the enhanced processing power AI machines can provide over humans to map it. The implications of this conclusion are vast and unending. You can't really argue against providing rights and ethics for AI if they are atomically no different to humans. Will there be a segregation between natural born and synthetic intelligence as there was between skin colours? Should we even allow AI to reach the same level of intelligence as humans considering they would not be bound by evolutionary limits as we are? Can AI become more intelligent than humans and what would that mean for mankind?

The Technological Singularity

Rise of the Robots

The technological singularity is perhaps the most widely discussed, and argued topic surrounding the rise of robotics and AI. Mathematically a singularity defines the point where a certain function becomes infinite such as the function 1/x. As we substitute for x tending towards 0, the function tends to infinity. This is how futurists and technologists are approaching the possible future development of AI. Developments in hardware and software will become ever more sophisticated and capable, making every future iteration increasingly more powerful. The logical conclusion here is that AI will at some point become "intelligent" enough to start programming and improving itself (without human input), initiating a runaway cycle of self-improvement far beyond our limited human intelligence can comprehend and therefore manage. The results of a situation like this are anyone's guess, but be rest assured it would result in an unfathomable change for humankind. If this occurs quicker than we can respond, we will be in danger of losing control. At this point, whether technology can ever be considered conscious or not is a mute point as man and machine will be indistinctive post-singularity.

Numerous experts in the field have been questioned regarding a possible date for this technology singularity, with the median year being (perhaps worryingly) 2040. One would have to take this value with a pinch (or perhaps a handful) of salt as the reasoning behind these estimates seem based on little more than random guesses. One might be tempted to simply pass off this subject as laughable, much like the Y2K bug panic in 2000. The possibility, however, should not be so quick to be dismissed, a thought shared by some of the most intelligent, capable and respected leaders in the AI field today. Stephen Hawking, Elon Musk and Bill Gates are among just a few who have openly expressed their concern with the uncontrolled rise of artificial intelligence, lending it at least some credibility.

Although AI has been on the technological landscape for quite some time, the recent rise of critics has coincided with notable developments in the field. Machine learning programs have made some surprising, if not worrying, innovations. Google's AlphaGo algorithm became the first program to beat a human professional player at Go, a game considered so complex it cannot be brute forced by calculating every move, as an unsophisticated computer would traditionally have to do. Instead, algorithms must "learn" the game and work out the best moves using strategy. Although seriously impressive, these deep learning programs are still very narrow and have no sense of true learning on a human scale. In terms of technology, effective "thinking" intelligence is still a way off, but in terms of time, it might come sooner than one thinks. That is the nature of a singularity, the progress is very small the further from the point of singularity, but progress is exponential and very rapid once a certain point is hit. Just because the technology is a long way off today, one mustn't underestimate the power of exponential progress.

Having concluded that it is scientifically possible for computer systems to be as intelligent as humans; the question of whether this event will actually occur is quite different but perhaps more important. The main issue that may very well stall the development of super intelligent AI is the physical hard technological barriers. Moore's Law describes how the number of transistors per square inch on an integrated circuit doubles approximately every two years. Although holding true for the past 40 years, the end is in sight for this Silicon Valley parable with only five more years of this progress estimated. The reason?

Transistors have now become so small we are hitting physical limits where mystifying quantum effects start to take hold. The current width of mass-produced chips is 14nm, but when considering this is just 70 times the width of a single silicon atom, the hard limit starts to become apparent. Although transistor densities are still increasing, the average clock speeds of regular computers (the speed at which a microprocessor executes instructions) hasn't significantly increased from around 2005 due to diminishing performance returns above clock speeds of 3GHz (a typical speed found in today's computers). Faster speeds build heat quite significantly, in turn adding costs in keeping it cool. The physical hard limits here create an economic barrier to continued progression. As with most engineering problems, with the right resources and incentives, they can usually be overcome. Although the physical limit for a silicon transistor is approaching, other tools and techniques such as doping silicon with other elements, using graphene, carbon nanotubes and multiple layered chips are all nascent technologies capable of pushing us through this barrier.

The physical limits are really indirect problems; although decreasing transistor size is no doubt a huge technological issue, the direct issue is the insurmountable costs of overcoming these issues. With enough R&D, new tools and techniques including the few mentioned above would, to some degree, be able to overcome these hurdles. The problem is justifying these huge investments. Since about 2012, physical phone sizes have actually started becoming larger due to greater consumer demand for larger screens to watch videos or read books. There is now a declining need to make phones, laptops etc. ever smaller when consumer demand is not there. Combine this with the eye-watering costs of developing and building smaller transistor fabrication plants and the return on investment diminishes significantly.

This effect is also comparable to hard drive storage sizes for iPods. In 2002 the average memory capacity was 10 gigabytes, doubling in the next year to 20GB, in 2004 40GB, 2006 80GB and 2007 160GB. This trend shows an approximate doubling in size every year. Extrapolating through to today (2018), the expected storage space for an iPod would be 328,000GB, 2500 times larger than a top capacity iPhone (it may not be realistic to assume storage size would reasonably double every year but the point remains valid). The reason this figure has not been achieved is not due to the lack of technology but a lack of consumer demand; 128GB is more than enough space for the average person's needs. The relevance here to AI is that exponentials can easily collapse when a lack of consumer demand slows progression, an effect which may very well prevent a technological singularity.

Lastly, we cannot underestimate society's role in making progress. Rightly or wrongly, society seems to be having a hard time adapting to even the most basic of AI, such as driverless cars, despite the consensus that they will probably be statistically safer than humans. AI medical diagnostics have proven to be more accurate than human doctors in areas where trawling through masses of data and finding relationships between them is advantageous for computers. Even knowing this many would still feel more comfortable having a second opinion from a carbon-based doctor. Although adoption is becoming ever more common (self checkouts in supermarkets and fast food restaurants) it is hard to visualise a time in the near future where mothers will happily allow robots to look after their newborns while they continue their professional careers unimpeded, or entrust their entire pension fund to an algorithm which is statistically proven to beat returns over human fund managers. Despite flying being statistically much safer than driving, we don't think twice about driving to the airport, getting on a plane, however, fills many with trepidation.

I hope the lack of a clear-cut answer regarding whether a technological singularity will occur doesn't disappoint, there are simply too many unknowns at this time that makes a decision impossible. Perhaps we will never know if there isn't an economic incentive to do so. Even so, the only wrong answer here to be ignorant of is the possible consequences and failure to prepare. For what would the world look like where humans are not the dominant intelligence?

One of Us

Brain vs. Brawn

Science fiction has long entranced its devoted readers with the prospect of a super- intelligence emerging as the dominant form of intelligence on earth. Stanislaw Lam's 1981 novel Golem XIV presents the scenario of how a seemingly well-intentioned military AI programme, which was programmed to aid its builders and prevent damages and loss of life due to war, became "self-aware". It concluded that warfare lacked internal logical consistency and thus becomes unresponsive. The reasons for this could be plentiful; the costs of war in terms of money, time and life may be greater than any benefits that would be realised. This would never be possible with human-level intelligence due to primal and ingrained human traits evolutionarily designed to be territorial and competitive. Replacing this human limit with a nonpartisan computer, however, and war perhaps becomes completely nonsensical, with the average quality of life for all involved reduced no matter which side emerges triumphant.

Perhaps the largest concern expressed by many (including the likes of Stephen Hawking, Bill Gates, and Elon Musk) is whether computers would be able to avoid being shut down if an algorithm started acting against societal norms. What if an algorithm, programmed to prevent environmental harm, calculates the ratio of humans to resources is unbalanced and seeks to rebalance this by reducing one side of the ratio? Resources can take decades to build up, with infrastructure such as hospitals very complex and expensive, so the logical course of action (for a computer of course) may be to reduce the human side of the ratio through a cull (potentially exploiting human susceptibility to biohazards or pandemics). It may sound far-fetched, but a computer hasn't any of the morals or ethics ingrained into humans through thousands of years of evolution. One could argue that coded into the algorithm would be a strict code of conduct with red lines that must not be crossed. But this may create a paradox; each year over 10 million people globally are killed as a result of pollution of some form. Logically, any solution an algorithm derives which results in fewer fatalities than 10 million will prevent net human loss of life, despite the solution perhaps involving intentional loss of life. In other words, a computer might come to the conclusion that the needs of the many outweigh the needs of the few, thus breaking its rule of avoiding harm to humans by obeying the very same rule it was instructed to follow.

Following on from this hypothetical situation, what if the results and solutions from this same algorithm were deemed unacceptable by societal norms and therefore ordered to be terminated? Being of an intelligence greater and thus not fully comprehensible to us, could the algorithm be in a position to decide that being switched off would result in failure of its primary instruction and therefore take measures to avoid a loss of power as a sub-goal? This situation is magnified with the ever increasing number of products which are digitally connected via the internet of things (IoT, see Chapter 3), where the number of resources a computer can pull from increases tremendously. At this point, AI would be out of human control and we would essentially be at its mercy.

No matter how optimistic one is regarding AI's approach to human life, it is difficult to see how human beings would not be considered a risk. Taking the magnificent, if not sombre, quote from Agent Smith (a super computer in human shape) in The Matrix film trilogy: "I'd like to share a revelation that I've had during my time here. It came to me when I tried to classify your species. I realized that you're not actually mammals. Every mammal on this planet instinctively develops a natural equilibrium with the surrounding environment, but you humans do not. You move to an area, and you multiply and multiply until every natural resource is consumed. The only way you can survive is to spread to another area. There is another organism on this planet that follows the same pattern: a virus. Human beings are a disease, a cancer of this planet. You are a plague, and we are the cure." This certainly highlights an element of truth; our higher level of self-awareness and intelligence allows us to see the damage we are doing to the planet, yet we carry on regardless because of our evolutionary instinct to think of ourselves first. Thus a super intelligence with this same awareness minus the individualistic need of humans would surely prioritise the planet (which the computer needs to survive and thus carry out its goals) over us. Essentially, humans are too much of a risk to the planet to not be exterminated, even if this is a "just on the safe side" approach.

Controlling this computer uprising, however, comes down to managing risk. Although computers eliminating mankind is a catastrophic hazard (something that can cause harm) if the risk (the chance of this hazard causing harm) is managed then severity may be controlled to a level where it is deemed an acceptable risk. For example, someone working at height inspecting the roof of a building will have the serious hazard of falling off the roof, with the risk being very high as a fall from even a few metres can kill. In the construction industry, we usually assign numbers (1-5 with 1 being low risk) to the severity and likelihood of a hazard. For this example, the severity of falling off a roof would be rated as a maximum of 5 (a fall from a few metres can kill), with the likelihood of the hazard occurring perhaps being a 4 (could be a fragile or slippery roof for example). Multiplying these together, we obtain a risk rating of 20, which is deemed too high to be carried out. Although the severity of a risk cannot usually be decreased, the likelihood can through control measures such as using some sort of safety harness and fall arrester. The likelihood of harm from falling is now reduced to perhaps 1, reducing the risk to 5x1 = 5, an acceptable level.

Applying this method to assessing risks from super intelligence, I would assign the risk from an AI takeover at the maximum 5 due to the possibility of causing mass harm to humanity, with the likelihood of the hazard occurring a subjective 3. This will be vastly disputed by various people, but I would argue anything greater than 1 is unacceptable because of the severity of the hazard. At a risk rating of 15, this is too great; we, therefore, need a way to lower the likelihood to a 1 to deem it acceptable. This is where the difficulty lies. Machine learning is the primary enabler of AI, allowing it to solve problems efficiently where brute force calculations would restrict, but the neural networks the algorithm creates are so vast they are very difficult to fully monitor. Creating systems to monitor and control the intelligent AI will be the key to successful implementation of intelligent AI systems.

Knowing all we know about the potential pitfalls of creating intelligent computers, would we be better off avoiding an AI takeover by preventing the creation of a super intelligence altogether? Surely it is unacceptable to introduce any risk involving the extinction of mankind no matter how small? I disagree, purely because there is so much to gain from creating super-intelligent machines. There are so many injustices and cruelties in the world which are purely logistical problems and which could be overcome through the use of intelligent systems, such as poverty, war, and disease. We cannot, in my opinion, stand by and allow these injustices to continue whilst having the capabilities to eliminate them.

By harnessing the power of intelligent machines some of the mysteries of the universe, such as the unfathomably complex processes behind quantum physics, might become solvable through the use of powerful neural networks. Unravelling and explaining these processes will open up a whole new level of technology, such as quantum entanglement and quantum teleportation. It may also help us finally explain the creation of the universe and help us identify whether we truly are alone or not.

A more immediate and perhaps more pressing development resulting from intelligent machine learning systems is a possibility of interplanetary travel and, as Elon Musk has dedicated his life to, interplanetary settlement. Drawing on Agent Smith's earlier quote, humanity is populating far too quickly for its resources. Despite many rich countries showing a decrease in population growth rates, this is far outweighed by growth in developing countries such as India and Africa. This growth will only continue as technology integrates itself further into society, especially in developing countries where economic growth and the elimination of poverty take precedence over environmental preservation. Unless policy and legislation change significantly globally, this is a one way trip down a road to an irreparable and uninhabitable planet, where the costs to counter the damage are greater than the cost to establish civilisations on other planets. Despite the cataclysmic outlook, humanity needs to at least be prepared for an event like this in the near(ish) future. Intelligent AI will be the key to not only exploring other planets (it is faster to pilot shuttles without humans on board) but also work out the necessary details and physics behind establishing civilisations, a topic so unfathomably complicated there might already be too little time for limited human intelligence to figure it out before it's too late.

AI may also prevent us from reaching this point of no return for the environment altogether. We can utilise the aforementioned lack of bias and selfish instinct to create environmental regulation that may well reverse the damage we have so far induced. Unfortunately, the biggest obstacle to this line of thinking will be government legislation; the lobbyist funds from oil companies are an influential aspect of today's politics. Unless some sort of social and environmental uprising overcomes this barrier, the chance to save our planet could very well pass us by.

Chapter Summary

We have so far explored how artificial intelligence may not one day be so artificial. Despite advocates of the hard problem of consciousness expressing their belief that human consciousness is a non physical entity and cannot be replicated, a compelling argument put forth by the likes of Dennett suggests consciousness is merely an illusion created by the brain, a result of evolutionary fine-tuning to make our lives simpler and more efficient i.e. competence without comprehension. Being a non-physical entity, the brain is made up simply of fundamental physical elements such as atoms and molecules. Our "consciousness" therefore, is merely the very complex and massive combinations of neurons and synapses, something which, in theory, could be replicated. The only difference is the basic building block; silicon vs carbon.

Even if the possibility of human and synthetic intelligence becoming indistinguishable was true, it does not mean to say it will happen. The common belief that a technological singularity where iterative self-improvement cycles are undertaken by machine intelligence, without human interference, will result in intelligent machines far beyond our understanding and control does not seriously consider the human effects that will no doubt slow this progress. Physical limits such as excessive heat buildup in smaller transistors may flatten the exponential effects of Moore's Law and slow the growth of clock rates in computers. The economic justification to keep shrinking and improving technology is governed by consumer demand, an effect shown by the lack of progress in memory capacities in iPods for example. Whilst weak AI provides strong economic incentives for advantageous sectors such as medical diagnosis and social media, there will be an equilibrium point where displaced jobs (and income), which have been replaced by automation, will result in a lack of consumer spending and therefore reduced demand for more automation, i.e. economics will dictate the pace of progress. Certainly, the 2040 date commonly whispered for an upcoming technological singularity seems rather unlikely.

This does not mean to say there is no need to prepare for the day AI becomes capable of making its own decisions. The results (although highly speculative) are existential; a computer whose only purpose is the completion of its task may well deem human beings as an unnecessary risk to its main resource, planet earth. Unbounded by human ethics and guided only by statistical logic, we cannot expect computers to share our common societal norms. We must therefore prepare, for failing to prepare is preparing to fail. Only by understanding a computers reasoning can we make informed decisions relating to risk, but with machine learning removing a lot of the reasoning from human control, we need to develop the tools and techniques to monitor their decisions.

Although the potential harm is high, we must not ignore the huge opportunities we stand to gain. Super intelligent systems could provide the power to reduce logistical problems ranging from poverty, disease, and war. We must be responsible for not only controlling AI but ensuring it is used to benefit mankind and minimise suffering.

In the near future, we should seek some form of alliance with artificial intelligence, combining the specialties from human intelligence such as common sense and interpersonal skills with the specialties from machine intelligence, such as trawling through masses of data at high speed and pattern recognition. This would aid innovation and boost productivity per person significantly, whilst also making our personal lives easier and more efficient. As long as we embrace AI safely and responsibly, it may be capable of pushing man through their natural limits of science and opening a whole other world we may have otherwise never realised.

"By far the greatest danger of Artificial Intelligence is that people conclude too early that they understand it."
Eliezer Yudkowsky

3.   Data and the Internet

Cloud Computing

Away with the clouds

Clouds are subtly mind-blowing. According to scientists, the average cumulus cloud weighs 1.1m pounds and floats above civilisation between 6,500ft and 45,000ft. Fortunately, clouds stay afloat because the water droplets are so small and spread over such a large distance that they have no appreciable fall velocity and stay suspended until the warm moist air cools and condenses to create rain. Cloud computing is no less impressive and will be as important to technical innovation as rain is to human existence.

Even to technophobes that have very little knowledge or interest in computing, the cloud has become synonymous with connectivity to computing resources anytime and anywhere. While computing is generally composed of storage (memory) and processors (power), cloud computing can accordingly be summarised as remote access to storage or processing power anytime and anywhere. All that is needed is an internet connection. Even if you have never had any direct involvement with cloud computing you have most likely used it if you have ever used an online service to send emails, stream movies, listen to music or save and share files online through the likes of Gmail, Netflix, Spotify, and Dropbox. In fact, this book, having been written on Google Docs whilst listening to Spotify (and occasionally whilst watching Netflix), wouldn't have been bought to you without the use of the cloud. So what's the big deal with the cloud and how will it affect you?

Cloud computing is another one of those innovations I class as "beautiful"; simplifying a complex process to enable rapid and easier innovation by others. An age-old scourge for almost all companies has been IT where companies, whether established or expanding, have had all manner of problems building and maintaining IT infrastructure. Rather than investing in expensive computers and all the associated infrastructure, companies can now, for a price, of course, rent access to a third party's array of servers and storage, remotely connected through the internet. This enables ubiquitous sharing of programs and information where the user avoids the upfront costs of personal computing infrastructure and pays only for what they use.

Unsurprisingly the usual suspects are leading the cloud computing charge. Amazon, Google, IBM, and Microsoft have all recently spent large sums in a bid to grab market share, with Microsoft committing 90% of its R&D budget to expand its cloud hosting capabilities. This investment has helped Microsoft increase its market share to 7%, ahead of Google's 2.3% but far behind Amazon's behemoth 44%. This vastly competitive industry is now worth nearly $250bn a year and compounding at 18% a year.

There is a whole host of reasons why individuals and businesses are switching their IT infrastructure to cloud models, mostly focusing around cost efficiencies. The upfront cost of infrastructure for an upstart can be understandably overwhelming; accurately gauging how much processing power and storage is needed before work starts is damn near impossible. Paying for access to someone else's infrastructure, therefore, avoids not only this often crippling upfront cost but other associated costs involved in operating and maintaining the infrastructure, such as the continuous running of on-site servers, round the clock electricity for power and cooling and IT experts for managing the infrastructure. All these are necessary for even the smallest of operations but soon add up to large sums, creating unnecessary barriers to entry purely due to logistical complexities.

The increase in flexibility afforded by the hiring of cloud computing can be a significant lifeline for many companies and the convenience and ease of use it presents often far outweighs the price premium. Typically, private IT infrastructures need to be scaled up to cope with worst-case scenarios, for example, an influx of users around peak times. I'm sure most of you have experienced first hand the infuriating task of trying to buy tickets to a music festival as they are listed, or trying to buy a lottery ticket for this year's biggest jackpot a couple of hours before the draw, with many websites unable to cope with this sudden and large increase in website visitors. Traditionally the solution to this problem has been to either scale up the infrastructure or simply accept the resulting poor service. The former is both expensive and wasteful as most of the capacity will sit idle and unused for most of the time and the latter results in lost sales. Cloud computing, however, allocates only the capacity that is needed at any specific moment, meaning the user doesn't have to worry about having either too little available capacity or too much, both expensively wasteful. This access to as little or as much capacity as is needed is made affordable by the economies of scale cloud providers can achieve and further enhances the flexibility for businesses as they can scale up seamlessly and match the pace at which they are growing, modifying their computing power, bandwidth and storage needs as they evolve, thus eliminating the need to keep buying new infrastructure whilst also avoiding the plague of having to constantly purchase new equipment as technology progresses. All this not only saves money directly but also increases performance, productivity and reliability whilst allowing its users to focus only on their core business and doing away with distractions which detract from the business's main priorities.

Cloud providers such as AWS (Amazon Web Services), Google Cloud and Microsoft's Azure offer various tiers of service for different needs. The common model provides three tiers often referred to as the cloud computing stack because each tier builds upon one another.

The first and most basic tier of cloud computing is referred to as Infrastructure as a service or IaaS (cloud computing terminology gets a bit strange) and offers the user the necessary infrastructure such as servers and virtual machines, storage, networks, firewalls/security and operating systems usually on a simple and flexible pay as you go type contract. It is the simplest tier and gains access to sheer computing power, the rest is up to the user. This is attractive and best suited to companies that want to build applications from the ground up and maintain maximum control of the development of the application whilst avoiding the pitfalls of buying and maintaining infrastructure which takes focus away from building their core product. Website hosting, storage, backup and recovery, access to HPC's (high-performance computing such as those used by universities) mostly utilise this tier where the economies of scale achieved by cloud providers provide plenty of processing power very economically.

Building upon this first tier is the Platform as a service model (PaaS) which incorporates all of the above but offers a few more services for those who need it. PaaS provides operating systems, development tools, database management, and business analytics to supply an on-demand environment for developing and publishing and managing software applications. Where PaaS differs from IaaS is by supporting web and app creators through all stages of the development process by offering middleware features such as software licenses and development tools, more suitable for smaller applications or companies that don't need the level of control that more specialist and generally larger companies need.

Finally, we have software as a service (SaaS) which, unsurprisingly, includes the infrastructure and platforms from the previous two tiers and adds another level of software to benefit those who have no interest in managing or owning infrastructure and operating platforms but care only for the use of an end product such as Gmail, Office 365 and Google Docs. Companies such as Microsoft and Google own and operate the entire infrastructure and simply provide a user interface for users to access over the internet. The tier of service required depends on the product or service the user provides and how much control they wish to maintain.

The benefits for companies are clear to see but what effect will cloud computing have on individuals? As technology starts to diverge away from Moore's Law and the rate of increase of clock speeds starts to decrease, devices such as computers and smartphones will struggle to keep pace with the ever-increasing demand from future power-hungry apps and services such as VR (virtual reality). There will be a point where it is cheaper or more preferable to "borrow" power from cloud computing servers, as opposed to internal processing power from the device internals. This means computers, smartphones, tablets, and many other devices will not need processors or internal memory storage as these needs will be outsourced to cloud servers. This would make personal devices faster, lighter, thinner, cheaper and vastly improve battery life; the main functions of these devices now morphs into information streaming via the internet from cloud servers and displaying this information through a display. Gone will be the days of yearly increases in RAM and clock speeds, replaced instead by battery life, screen resolution, and sleekness.

This transition from hardware to software will be gradual; however, as cloud adoption is limited by internet connectivity and speeds which require substantial infrastructure investments. We are already seeing a shift towards cloud use; much of the television and music watched and listened to is streamed. Most of a user's personal information is saved and recoverable from the cloud (for better or worse) and so much of the convenience offered by modern-day computing is made possible through cloud computing. Our rapid increase in dependence on cloud servers in just a few years merely goes to show just how seamless and useful the cloud is. It may not be long before we have essentially unlimited power in the palm of our hands.

Connectivity

Too Much Information

Perhaps one of the biggest global injustices to date is the fact that two-thirds of the world's population still doesn't have access to the internet. Direct investment in clean water, malaria, HIV or aid for conflict may at first glance appear more important (they are certainly direct sources of immense suffering) but whereas this sort of direct aid proves mostly temporary or small scale, the infusion of permanent access to any information anytime and anywhere would tackle these issues at the source and help people to help themselves.

According to the World Economic Forum, only 20.7% of Africa's population use the internet, compared to 77.6% for Europe, mostly due to a lack of availability or affordability. Broadband boosts economic growth in all countries but developing countries have the most to gain. A 2009 Information and Communications report by the World Bank showed that for every 10 points of broadband connection in developing countries, GDP grew by 1.35% compared with a still impressive 1.21% for developed countries.

There are a myriad of reasons why internet connectivity improves the quality of lives. A study in the journal Science has found that internet mobile banking app, M-Pesa, in Kenya has helped lift 194,000 families or 2% of households, out of poverty between 2008 and 2014 and now has 17.6m active users, representing at least one user in 96% of Kenyan households. Mobile banking apps avoid the expensive burden of building brick and mortar banks where cash has to be physically drawn and deposited, especially expensive in developing countries which the majority of residents are overwhelmingly rural. Even developed countries with mature banking industries are closing more and more of their branches as a new wave of savvy internet users now use online banking for 54% of their payments, resulting in a 32% decline in visits to physical banks. This has created a few online-only banking firms such as Fidor, First Direct and Revolut who can offer better interest rates through their lower operating costs. Users in developing countries can send money to friends and family members far away for access to medicine, school fees, and books. Most workers in developing countries get paid inconsistently and with cash or services which often remain untracked and off the government radar. Reliable online banking, however, allows for salaries and income to be tracked and accounted for, allowing states to better identify and collect taxable income which could be used to improve services for citizens.

As well as making payments, safer, cheaper and faster, being connected also allows for a flow of information to those who would otherwise struggle to educate themselves. Developing countries are surprisingly more likely to use social media then developing countries. 86% of users in the Middle East, 82% of Latin America and 76% of African users regularly visit social media sites such as Facebook and Twitter compared to 71% in the US and 65% of Europeans. This shows the demand for knowledge and awareness of political situations in countries often involved in political dissent where authoritarianism and corruption is suppressing political freedom in crony states. The prosperity of true successful democracy depends on access to accurate and correct information. A lack of this, however, leads to autocratic propaganda and the rise of dictatorships.

Wireless Connections

From clouds to cables

Of course is it not as simple as building the infrastructure to realise the immediate benefits from mass internet connectivity; the internet is still of little use for those who can't read and write. There are also many who can't afford it. But whilst internet connectivity will continue to increase, the traditional model of cable connections may shift towards a more wireless model. Similar to how nascent online banks (and now even traditional banks) are benefiting from shifting to online-only models, cellular data providers could also reach millions of new customers without the burden of having to build expensive cabled networks which can take decades to build. Mobile networks such as 3G and 4G have changed the wireless game and the next iteration, 5G, will further the use of such mobile networks whilst also providing opportunities for further innovations.

With the introduction of 3G and 4G networks came an explosion in the use of network traffic as millions of users benefited from ubiquitous access to information. In 2017, internet traffic from mobile devices hit 50% of all traffic, up 20% from just 2 years prior. An increase in online shopping has also corresponded with this hike, a direct result of the speed and convenience offered by fast mobile networks. Businesses can now Skype and conference call anytime and anywhere, increasing efficiency and productivity. Real-time GPS and navigation systems have also become a possibility through faster speeds, enabling mobile devices to replace traditional satnav systems and providing benefits to many users such as delivery companies and the emergency services. Whilst the 4G network has kept pace with societal demands for 6 years now, the demands from new bandwidth-intensive applications such as video stream-ing services and the upcoming surge of the Internet of Things (see next sec-tion) are clogging up the limited frequency spectrum. 5G, the next iteration in wireless communications, could be the means to connect this wealth of new information with its users.

As you would expect from a new iteration, 5G will be faster than its predecessor by 20 times peak speed and at least a factor of 10 when looking at real-world performance. As mentioned previously, the frequency 5G transmitted over will be higher than the 2GHz that is currently used by 4G. Higher frequencies will be beneficial for multiple reasons, the first being that they support a much larger bandwidth capacity resulting in much faster speeds. This new spectrum is not only less cluttered from all the existing networks used in the lower frequencies but the waves themselves are highly directional and reduce the interference from other devices. This is a vast improvement on 4G transmission towers which beam radio waves in any and every direction even if they aren't needed. These highly directionalised waves will be able to support 1000 more devices per meter than what is currently possible with 4G. For end users, this results in an ultra-fast performance with little latency and high precision. It is not all plain sailing; however, there are some technicalities to first overcome. Higher frequencies afford a greater network capacity but do not travel as far as lower frequencies and are not as good at passing through obstacles, ultimately reducing the effective range of the transmitted waves. Technologies and techniques are being developed to reduce the severity of these issues but less range means more transmitter stations, inevitably increasing the cost to build the new 5G network.

Infrastructure such as masts and transmission towers will only be part of the costs. In April 2018, the UK auctioned off some of the spectrum necessary for hosting the 5G network. The network operator O2 acquired the largest portion of this spectrum, paying a mammoth £206 million for 40MHz of the 2.3GHz spectrum and £318 for 40MHz of the higher 3.4GHz frequency. EE and Vodafone also won some other frequencies; in total, Ofcom auctioned 190MHz of spectrum in the 2.3GHz to 3.4GHz range.

The fact that the frequencies have only just been dished out reminds us that 5G is still a way off from commercial introduction. We can expect to see the wave of 5G rollout around 2020, with full deployment in 2025 at the earliest. It will be critical to have a high-speed communications network for the successful and widespread development of autonomous vehicles which rely on low latency connections to operate quickly enough to keep up with traffic algorithms. The internet of things will also create millions of more devices each needing an internet connection to transmit the resulting masses of data which would quickly overwhelm and degrade current infrastructure and degrade its service. It is important to also think about the needs of developing countries that will need an infrastructure capable enough to keep its ever-growing number of mobile users connected.

As to whether mobile networks will result in the demise of cabled networks such as copper and fibre optic cables altogether is unlikely. Huge sums have been invested and high-quality fibre optics can offer greater speeds and latency than 5G networks. Cabled Wi-Fi also provides service to those hard to reach places such as basements that mobile networks will always struggle to reach. As with many new technologies, a combination of both wired and wireless networks will maximise the benefits to consumers. Rural areas may benefit from an introduction to 5G networks where terrestrial cabled networks are not cost effective. Although more expensive than cables, government legislations and targets of reaching set broadband speeds for all households may be able to subsidise costs or perhaps set a minimum cost per Mbps that providers must make available.

Looking much further ahead in time, Elon Musk has once again provided an audacious, if not impressive, proposition of covering the entire planet with gigabit internet (a minimum download speed of up to 1Gbps, about 50 times today's average of about 20Mbps) by a complicated system of around 12,000 satellites orbiting the planet in synergy. Little is known or has been said about this ambitious project but on February 22nd, 2018 SpaceX's Falcon 9 rocket launched into space releasing 2 prototype satellites named Microsat-2a and Microsat-2b into the orbit for testing. Eventually, the massive network of 12,000 satellites orbiting at various altitudes will be able to cover the entire planet and provide internet access to anyone, anytime and anywhere. The company expects in excess of 40 million subscribers by 2025 (If this claim is anything like Mr. Musk's claims for Tesla Model 3 production, however, we can take this with a pinch of salt). The ability to cover the whole globe with wireless internet would be of immense value; the ability to avoid the huge financial commitments of building and maintaining a vast cabled internet network would accelerate uptake in developing countries by a huge margin. In the meantime, superfast 5G networks will have to suffice.

Internet of Things, IoT

One Thing Leads to Another

The internet of things (IoT) is a strange term but one which does exactly what it says on the tin; it is the interconnectivity of internet-connected devices enabling information to be seamlessly shared between them for maximum efficiency. Legal scholars suggest thinking of the "thing" aspect as an inextricable synergistic mixture of hardware, software, data, and service. Essentially the IoT allows a plethora of devices to be remotely sensed or controlled through the internet to create a network of devices which can collect, share and act upon information. By connecting devices such as washing machines, sinks, light bulbs, and kettles, the IoT becomes a sort of middleman between the previously untapped offline world and the online realm, collecting masses of data for offline tasks which can potentially help both consumer and producer to create and use better products and services.

The first wave of IoT connected devices could be considered a bit of a fad. From fridges which inform you of dwindling milk supplies to coffee makers which sync with your alarm to brew a fresh cup of Joe upon waking up, these inventions are hardly going to change the world. With time and experience, however, has come more useful innovations such as smart thermostats which are enabling households globally to become more efficient, reducing both the carbon footprint and the cost to consumer's pockets. Nest is currently one of the market leaders in this field and uses algorithms to learn of a household's routine, automatically adjusting the temperature needs of each individual home in the most efficient manner possible according to the occupier's personal circumstances. Savings to household bills from such systems save an average of 20%. When outside temperatures drop below freezing the heating will automatically adjust to stop the pipes freezing and likewise, when it's hot you can inform the app of your arrival home in order to preset the air conditioning so you can arrive home to a perfectly acclimated home without having to have had the cooling on all day. Although this may not seem revolutionary on an individual scale, the cumulative impacts when applied globally to millions of households would be incredible, significantly reducing the carbon footprint from buildings, saving users money and significantly reducing and energy demands from power plants.

Even the most innocent of inventions, the key, will soon be fired straight into antiquity. The first recorded use of a pin type lock has been traced to 704 BC and has nobly been serving society's security needs ever since. Smart locks are becoming increasingly popular as wearable's such as smart watches and mobile phones replace the traditional key and allow access to whoever the owner wishes to grant access to. It is not just individuals and households who stand to benefit, businesses have jumped head first into the field to realise the commercial benefits of such tech. Shipping company DHL is experimenting with technology which utilises IoT technology, such as vehicle monitoring and maintenance, sensors in shipping containers, real-time tracking of packages and tracking of employee movements, in a bid to realise efficiency gains over its competitors in this growing but hugely competitive field.

IoT connected products and services are not just valuable for companies because of their product profit margins. A secondary value will be placed on the user data the products collects which is currently the property of the company selling the product. The integration of devices which stream non stop data from millions of users is a non-intrusive way for companies to obtain what was once private and offline data. For some devices the data generated may indeed be more valuable than the product itself, perhaps creating the possibility of heavily subsidised or even free appliances in exchange for the data it generates.

There is truly no limit to the sort of devices that can be connected and we will see waves of innovations and start-ups utilising this technology. Some of the immediate beneficiaries will be industries like healthcare, agriculture, and infrastructure where mass data would enable clear identification of patterns and trends and therefore make accurate statistical predictions. Healthcare is one of the most exciting and promising industries which could be revolutionised into a new era of mass efficiency. Wearable tech such as smartwatches are already becoming hugely popular with an estimated one in six consumers already owning such an item. Market leaders such as Apple and Fitbit can track heart rate, movement, sleep and calories burned, helping users take an informed lead in improving their own health. Taken further, these items, and later internal body sensors such as pacemakers, may allow for real-time monitoring of blood pressure, oxygen levels and blood cell count to automatically and immediately alert the relevant medical personnel of a potential issue, such as strokes and heart attacks, the likes of which become significantly more damaging the longer they remain untreated. Knowledge like this will allow medicine and healthcare to become more proactive as opposed to the current reactive healthcare model, offering significant benefits to all involved. Great Britain's NHS is already stretched thin financially in part due to the increase in life expectancy where over two-fifths of NHS spending is directed at over 65s. Knowing the vitals of the elderly may enable paramedics to remotely diagnose problems such as low blood sugar levels or heart rates to potentially avoid expensive ambulance trips that might not be necessary.

Medical institutions are not the only beneficiaries. Medical insurers have long had to base their quotes on the fact that the young end up subsidising the old and the healthy, the more ill-prone. Just like how black boxes on vehicles measure how safely the operator drives to tailor the quote to the individual driver, wearable tech allows insurers to build up a personal profile of an individual to allow for a more informed and subjective quote, potentially lowering premiums for the healthier. Insurance costs, in general, should also fall as the tech is generally expected to reduce both the number of medical issues and their severity. This saving combined with government subsidies could go part of the way to subsidising those individuals whose premiums are expected to increase upon being found a higher risk for insurers based on the collected data. Seeing as the wallet is usually the most effective driver of change, the prospect of cheaper insurance should entice the majority to shape up and live healthier lives.

We can expect cities to become much "smarter" and edge closer to the "Big Brother" image of sci-fi cities monitoring their inhabitants. In Britain, councils are experimenting with infrastructure such as street lighting which turns on extra bright when sensing shouting or hollering such as in a mugging situation, alerting nearby cameras to track those who are in the area. Traffic lights with sensors are also becoming more common where computer algorithms track and monitor traffic flows in a bid to avoid cars sitting idle at traffic lights, which is responsible for 17% of the fuel burned in urban areas.

With a deeper and subtler integration of technology into society comes deeper suspicions and concerns regarding how much of our privacy we can hold onto. The fact that so much information will be transferred without human input means the IoT could simply fade into the background and remain hidden from view. There are also concerns of an "always on" world as devices which need an internet connection to function will cease to operate without a live connection. This hyperconnected network poses problems for those who wish to go off the grid or live in rural areas. A digital divide may occur between those who have access to constant internet and those who do not. There is also the concern of passing more influence to companies selling IoT devices and collecting its associated data. The lack of clarity about where the data goes and who has access to it will also need to be addressed amid security concerns; imagine a burglar hacking or obtaining a live feed from your security cameras to assess when the house is empty. As with most upcoming tech, these concerns are certainly valid but with proper planning and further technological advances, they can be overcome. There is much to gain from a world of information connected in real time, from automated cars to avoiding a heart attack; the IoT will continue to infiltrate our lives. New upstarts will use the technology for purposes perhaps unimaginable to us today. But public adoption will only grow so far if the associated security and privacy concerns are not addressed alongside them. This nicely takes us to the next topic; data and privacy.

Data

Safety Net

Now has never been a more apt time to discuss the future of data and the rights to privacy for those who produce it. The last few years have given rise to a few mammoth data breaches from huge corporate goliaths one would think to be the most secure. Yahoo has had a number of embarrassing breaches such as the 2014 compromising of 500 million user's real names, dates of birth, telephone numbers and even addresses, enough information to cause serious issues from anyone with intent. This was only a matter of months after Yahoo had a similar breach in 2013 which compromised a staggering 1 billion accounts (reports now put the real number closer to 3 billion). Perhaps more seriously, Equifax in July 2017 saw hackers obtain 143 million user's social security numbers, names, addresses, and driver's license numbers as well as 209,000 credit card details. The reason for so many cyber attacks? Data is a very lucrative business and companies are not the only ones looking to gain from it; criminals can bypass the already very loose rules and regulations to make a quick buck.

Research from Malwarebytes, a computer security firm, found 40% of companies from a sample of 500 across 4 countries had experienced a ransomware attack and a third of these reported losing revenue as a result. In the UK this was as high as 54%. A fifth of affected British companies reported being charged over $10,000 for access to their computer systems to be regained and 3% over $50,000. Perhaps more worrying is the fifth of companies who were ransomed for less than $500, a small price to pay in the pragmatic world of business where every hour out of action could cost thousands. This explains why around half of the companies eventually paid up and also why the issue is an ongoing and growing problem; the lure of quick and easy money without having to come face to face is ideal for criminals.

The rise in cybercrime is also an inevitable result of an exponential increase of data in general. An IBM Marketing Cloud study found that 90% of all data on the internet has been created since 2016 thanks in part not only to the rise of data generating and collecting hardware such as phones, computers, watches, parking meters etc. but also to better and more thorough algorithms and software aimed at better creation, collection and analysis of data. By 2020 this stands to rise to 40 zettabytes of information, an unfathomably large number which American linguist Mark Liberman estimates is close to the storage requirements for recording all human speech ever spoken if digitized as 16 kHz 16-bit audio. Social media has played a very large part of this rise, with reports from "Digital in 2017" showing that social media gains 840 new users each minute, that's 14 every second or 3.5 times the number of births per second. The same study presents the scale of development through eye-opening statistics (in 2017); 4,146,600 videos watched every minute, 3,607,080 Google searches every minute and 5.97 billion hours of YouTube videos watched each day. These numbers are so large it is hard to grasp the magnitude of content available but starts to put into context the sheer quantity of information available to those who are able to collect it.

The reason for this strong push towards data collection and storage is ultimately simple; it is of massive value for those who can utilise it. "Big Data" is the term used to refer to these extremely large datasets which can then be analysed computationally to predict trends and patterns especially relating to human behaviour. Retail industries find it of particular value as it allows companies to identify and target specific consumers much more efficiently and therefore profitably. Whilst browsing the web on your computer for new clothes, for instance, Google's algorithms will be building up a profile of you and can group you into a cluster of consumers who are searching for clothes. Google can now better target its ads for clothing companies when buying advertising through Google, hopefully resulting in a win for all parties involved; Google earns revenue from advertisers who pay for their ad to appear, websites hosting the ads earn whenever someone clicks an ad, the advertiser wins whenever the advertised product or service is purchased and the consumer wins by purchasing something which (hopefully) adds value to their life. It, therefore, follows that the better these ads are at targeting the consumer the higher the sales for the advertiser and the more Google can earn from either higher priced ads or simply more of them as the sales results tempt more companies into purchasing ads. This process has been the primary use and value of data for the past decade or so but the value of data is increasing as companies such as Google are finding more uses for the information which will generate new sources of revenue. Artificial intelligence can now provide services such as translation, visual recognition and assessing personality and behaviour, all of which could be sold to other companies for purposes perhaps not even known yet.

Tesla is an example of a company which is collecting masses of data with the aim of improving its own products; the sensors in its electric vehicles are collecting all sorts of telematics such as time driven, speed, braking distances, reactions to emergencies and many others with the aim of improving its autopilot system. By the end of 2016, Tesla vehicles had amounted 1.3bn miles worth of data surpassing Waymo's and Alpahabet's miles by orders of magnitude. Uber's $51 billion value is not just a direct value of its ride hailing services but is also partly a result of the value of the data it holds as shown by the sale of its data to city planners who can use the information to better plan its infrastructure needs. Although Facebook may be free in terms of payments, the price we pay is actually in the consent we give for our data to be collected and sold to advertisers. In light of recent events involving Facebook, Cambridge Analytica and the abuse of masses of personal data, many users are becoming much more attentive of their digital footprint, meaning the current model of free usage in exchange for data may soon wear thin.

You may be curious to know just how much your data is quantifiably worth. There are a host of websites which sell targeted data to those who have a need for it; ExactData.com is one such website which offers a bundle of data of 1.8 million names, addresses, cities, states, and ZIP codes all for a one-off sum of $138,380 or just 7.5 cents a person. The Times newspaper did a similar study and calculated a similar price of 8 cents per person, increasing slightly for homeowners or the ill, presumably as they are easier to sell to. Traditional methods of selling data are private negotiations such as that mentioned above with ExactData.com and the private sale between Uber and city planners. This model has typically been vulnerable to abuse as regulation is minimal and deals are private. This too is soon set to change as the industry matures and better organisation emerges. Data exchanges are now being set up where, similar to commodities and shares, data can be bought and sold by those who value it the most. Fetch is one of the emerging leaders in the field and aims to match data queries from those who need it (a coffee shop, for instance, may request information on local spending habits and disposable income for instance) and other companies with such information can satisfy this data request for a price. This will also benefit large companies with large private data collections which may be sitting idle on private servers. Fetch hopes to launch in 2019.

Privacy

iSpy

We have seen so far why data is so valuable and how those collecting, analysing and benefitting from it have mostly been businesses and corporations seeking profits. But where does this data collection leave those from whom the data was collected and where do they stand legally and ethically? It is important to remember that the data itself is not the problem; the many innovations already mentioned such as the IoT, cloud computing and widespread connectivity all stand to greatly improve the quality of life for those who use it. How and by whom this data is used is what causes ethical concern and in light of the many cases of abuse of data, regulations, and codes of conduct need to be introduced to protect those unable to protect themselves.

Near the top of the list of ethical concerns is the potential for a huge database and profile build of anyone and everyone who leaves a digital footprint. We already know personal details such as name, address, and email are collected and shared by those who aim to tailor specific adverts to consumers. But what if this goes a step further? What if a failed payment on a mortgage or phone bill, even for the most genuine of reasons, categorised you as a late payer and affected your future credit status? China already has an extensive database of its citizen's details, which includes a near exhausted collection of photographs, and has attempted to create a "citizen score" used to determine eligibility for loans, employment, and travel visas. In an autocratic state like

China where freedom of speech is suppressed, the amount of power the state could exert with this knowledge is truly terrifying.

Cambridge Analytica's controversial influences over recent major events such as Brexit and the US presidential election in 2016 have brought to light the consequences of what happens when too much data is utilised without proper and thorough regulation. Cambridge Analytica had started collecting data on Facebook users since 2014 via a personality app. Cambridge Analytica used the 300,000 people who downloaded the app to pull further information from their friends via Facebook's' Graph API interface, through which third parties can interact with Facebook's' platform. In all an estimated 87 million users are thought to have had their personal data collected by Cambridge Analytica from Facebook alone. They also claim on their own website that they hold over 5000 data collection points on each of 230 million Americans. This proved enough information to build psychological profiles of millions of people to target political messages with the aim of swaying political opinion, a great cause of concern in a nation which prides itself as a flag-bearer for democracy. Cambridge Analytica claim they always acted within the law. Even if this were true, there is surely a huge ethical concern when using bots to spread news and fake stories. The company has since closed down due to both existing and new clients avoiding a company of such hysterical news but have covertly launched under the new company name of Emerdata. The damage has been done, however. Facebook CEO, Mark Zuckerberg, testified before the Congress over the breach of data and has admitted his part in the lack of protection and control of its collected data to prevent political manipulation and has since vowed to tighten user's control of data. This is the first real meaningful pushback against these big data giants and has opened both individual user's and government's eyes to the power wielded by those with access to big data and therefore the start of regulation to control it.

Fortunately for the average Joe, there is hope on the horizon. Europe has recently passed through a new set of regulations which will help protect the data of its citizens and give them more control and access to what is and isn't shared online. The GDPR (General Data Protection Regulation) law replaces the antiquated and no longer relevant existing data protection laws created in the 1990's with a new and up to date set of procedures and standards designed to harmonise data protection laws across Europe and give greater protection and rights to individuals. Among some of the main features is the need for parental permission to purchase data on children under 16, easier access to individuals collected and stored data (the current £10 Subject Access Request will now be free of charge) as well as predefined fines for breaking of any of these rules. The UK's ICO (Information Commissioner's Office) can currently wield a maximum fine of up to £500,000. The new GDPR rules will raise this to a maximum of €10 million or 2% of a firm's total revenue for lesser offenses, rising to €20 million or 4% of a firm's maximum revenue for more serious offenses; significant sums which should raise the priorities for businesses about their data security. Within mere hours of the introduction of the GDPR laws, complaints were launched about Google, Facebook, Instagram and WhatsApp for forcing users to accept terms and conditions outside of the law. Potential fines could more than to $3m each.

Individuals now have the power to get their personal data withdrawn under certain circumstances such as where the data is no longer necessary for the purpose it was collected for, there's no legitimate interest to hold the data or if it was unlawfully processed. Although a European Law this will affect any company which processes a European citizen's data regardless of geography, meaning even American firms such as Netflix will need to abide by the rules for its European customers. Despite Brexit, the UK is still expected to adopt the policy for all its citizens. It is only a matter of time before the US pushes through a similar law as the tech behemoths fall out of favour with politicians, their lobbying power declines and public sentiment surrounding data privacy grows.

Net Neutrality

A Web of Lies

Our final chapter on this topic will look at Net Neutrality and its preservation. This has been a hugely debated and controversial topic of late not just because of its immediate implications but also because of its deeper proxy as a voice for the masses against the elite. Net neutrality does exactly what it says on the tin; it is the idea that all information on the internet is neutral, equally accessible with no discrimination or different charges by user, content, website etc. More specifically, internet service providers (ISPs) cannot intentionally block, slow down or charge money for specific websites or online content.

The common analogy for explaining how ISPs are trying to rework how internet data is broadcasted is through lanes of traffic. Think of the current system as cars (data) travelling to their destination (our devices) via a single lane of traffic. As there is only one lane there is no overtaking, therefore each packet of data travels at the same speed behind the one it is following and no packet has priority over another; it is a first come first serve basis. ISPs have realised that by creating more lanes they can move selected packets faster than others by allowing them to overtake in a metaphoric fast lane, for a fee of course. The problem lies with the potential control ISPs could then wield over what we see online, slowing and perhaps blocking entirely anything that hasn't been given priority by those who have coughed up, or simply content which conflicts with their private interests. An immediate concern would be content dominance by the bigger corporations who can afford it such as Google, Amazon, and Facebook. Smaller companies trying to break through would be severely hindered by simple economics as they struggle to compete with the incumbents, reducing competition, innovation and ultimately reducing value for the consumer. Facebook itself would never have developed from an idea in Mark Zuckerberg's College dorm to defeating the Goliath MySpace without the freedom and opportunity afforded by net neutrality.

For consumers, a loss of net neutrality would inevitably (although probably not immediately) result in paywalls for access to different content online. Although bound by European net neutrality rules, Portugal allows for certain kinds of pricing schemes that give a picture of an internet unbound by net neutrality. The wireless carrier MEO offers (on top of a base contract) packages for messaging (WhatsApp, Skype, Facetime), social media (Facebook, Twitter, Instagram), Video (Youtube, Netflix) and music all for an extra $4.99 a month for each package. Although these are currently only optional packages providing unlimited data for these specific applications, the concern is the possibility of various US opponents to net neutrality using this system as a viable model for accessing (or blocking) certain online content in the future.

Unsurprisingly, those who are trying to appeal the net neutrality model and transfer to a restricted access model are the ISP providers themselves and the FCC (US Federal Communications Commission). Their first argument is the increased revenues earned from tiered packages would be used to fund better access to rural customers whose expensive setups are not cost-efficient for ISPs. The improvement of ISP's infrastructures will also help them fix their outdated business models. Broadband packages are normally priced mostly by speeds, such as $9.99 for unlimited broadband up to a speed of 100Mbps. Although you have paid for 100Mbps you will very rarely achieve this because the infrastructure behind it is unable to deliver this speed to all its customers simultaneously. ISPs use a model such as 200:1; 200 people sharing a single line based on the assumption that not everyone will be using the connection simultaneously. This model was adequate at a time where the majority of broadband use was simple browsing which uses minimal bandwidth for short periods of time. Since bandwidth intensive apps such as Netflix and peer to peer content sharing sites have become popular, the 200:1 model is now insufficient and unfit for purpose. Streaming from Netflix is responsible for ⅓ of all internet bandwidth, followed by YouTube with ⊠, combining to become responsible for a staggering ½ of all bandwidth consumed on the internet. ISPs, therefore, argue that those who use the most bandwidth should have to pay the most in the form of purchases such as video streaming bundles. This is a valid point and is no different to the pay per minute phone contracts or pay per mile taxis happily accepted today. The reason for the mass outrage against the ISPs and FCC is not so much the concept but the lack of trust and the conflict of interest between businesses (profit) and that of the public (a fair, free and unrestricted platform). ISPs have already been given government subsidies and have had money set aside for improving the infrastructure but there has been little to show for it, most companies essentially pocketed it. Capitalist businesses since time immemorial have been transient and constantly fight for survival as the world around them changes and they evolve to survive, a system which benefits the consumer with fair priced products and services resulting from a competitive environment. Blockbuster, Kodiak, Yahoo, and Xerox are a just a few of the many thousands of companies that have failed to innovate and paid the price; they never received any help from government subsidies so why should ISPs? Any company which cannot foresee future demand and keeps up with their environment should be replaced by companies which are more competitive and innovative; this is the basis of democratic capitalism that has seen developed countries prosper. Why should ISPs be any different?

Perhaps most important is the preservation of online free speech and access to accurate information. By handing ISPs the ability to control what information flows where and when, we risk information flow being controlled by money. Those parties who can afford to pay more to prioritise their content using these fast lanes will now have a larger control over what information its users see. Whilst many of these fast lane users will use it for innocent enough business use, it is inevitable that there will be those who misuse it as a way to push their partisan agendas. This is especially prevalent in an age of political meddling, such as the recent spread of fake news and Russian meddling in the 2016 US presidential election. A fair democracy can only truly be fair in an environment where access to information is equal and free, two criteria which will quickly disappear once a paywall is introduced

Almost all arguments in favour of net neutrality focus around the worry of placing so much power and trust in the hands of just a few whose objectives of maximising profit go directly against the premise of fair and equal access to the internet for all. Without it, the wave of internet innovations that has benefitted us all over the last couple of decades will be at risk of slowing significantly. As of writing (May 2018), the US Senate proposed to restore net neutrality thanks to the hugely active and impressive pushback from the general public. This will be a constant battle as lobbyists and Republican elites try to appeal neutrality and represent a larger proxy for the rise of populist beliefs against the often selfish elite. Watch this space.

Summary

American entrepreneur Mitchell Kapor once quipped that "getting information off the internet is just like taking a drink from a fire hydrant". The amount of information the internet makes available and its resulting potential to benefit mankind is truly staggering and will only continue to grow at a terrific rate. Remaining in control and utilising all this information in the best and most useful manner will require cogent planning and legislation to keep up with the rate of change, something which has not occurred in the short history of the internet to date.

Cloud computing is one of many innovations set to change the digital landscape. Businesses will be the most immediate beneficiary as their expensive and cumbersome IT systems are replaced with swift and dynamic outsourced cloud networks, reducing operating costs for established companies and removing a tricky barrier for start-ups who can seamlessly adapt and scale with the momentum of the business. Cloud networking may soon find its way into mainstream technology too, outsourcing the bulky and expensive processing and storage components in devices to the large and efficient cloud servers and simply streaming it through the internet to your device. The capabilities of modern devices such as smartphones, watches, and implants will have potentially unlimited power, restricted only by the speed and reliability of the transmission network.

To cope with these new transmission demands, incumbent wireless networks will have to be upgraded or replaced. 5G currently offers the most promising option with tech-savvy countries such as South Korea, who aim to commercialise the technology as early as March 2019, leading the charge. Although 5G offers up to ten times the real world speed as the current 4G system, the higher frequency of these new systems will require an expensive infrastructural overhaul. The demands for a faster and more reliable network should make this investment more than viable, however, as the demands from future IoT connected devices will increase significantly.

It is not only rich countries with their wealth of new technologies that stand to gain the most, however. Developing countries have already benefited tremendously from the recent penetration of mobile connectivity, with online digital banks allowing for quicker and more secure forms of payment than traditional brick and mortar banks could ever allow for. Mobile data also allows for the complete bypassing of traditional networks of copper and fibre cables whose installation and maintenance are expensive and slow. Further promoting the spread of mobile devices and networks should remain a priority for both governments and charities as the ability to help others to help themselves will always be more efficient then one-off aid.

Looking longer term, however, rumours abound of a global network for connecting everyone on the planet to a basic quality of internet access. From Google's balloon satellites to Elon Musk's gigabit satellites, the ambitious if not slightly wacky ideas are noble in thought and the goal of bringing a minimum quality of internet connectivity to each and every person is one that certainly needs pursuing.

Whilst new technology and faster computing is continuing to innovate like never before, governance of such powerful systems and its corresponding data must also keep pace. The potential profits offered by big data have now turned it into a global commodity, with businesses globally paying greater and greater sums with hopes of converting this data into profit. A lack of clear regulation and oversight in the big data industry has inevitably resulted in the scandals of late, such as the exploitation of data by Cambridge Analytica and the resulting political meddling in the 2016 presidential election.

Years of loose oversight may now finally be starting to come under control. The noble GDPR rules from Europe has handed back at least some control of user's data and revamped punishments for those who fail to comply. Whether they go far enough to prevent the exploitation of those who own the data, however, remains to be seen.

More fundamental to the prosperity of the internet, however, is the preservation of the core values which has given rise to all that has been achieved today. Net neutrality is essential to ensuring the content and information we see remains in line with the values of democracy. Allowing ISPs the ability to charge more for different content introduces the potential for information manipulation; those with the means to pay can affect how and what the general internet public see. Though arguments for and against net neutrality certainly have their place; the fundamental democratic values of accurate and equal access to information must be protected at all costs, especially in times of political interference and populist uprisings around the world testing the very nature of democracy as a whole. For if we are to continue to prosper from the fruits of successful democracy which has benefitted the Western world to today, we must continue to participate and fight for its protection.

4. Transportation

Stepping up a Gear

Autonomous Vehicles (AVs) have been a staple of science fiction films for decades and usually denote a utopian era of innovation, minimalism, efficiency, and style. Minority Report (2002) showed densely packed autonomous pods ebbing in and out of traffic within inches of others at breakneck speeds whilst navigating multiple lanes and criss-crossing roads in such a seemingly complex series of manoeuvres it makes driving in Manhattan rush hour look like a Sunday stroll in the park. Total Recall (1990) featured Arnold Schwarzenegger riding in "Johnny Cabs"; autonomous taxis which somewhat resemble today's Uber - minus the simultaneously friendly and creepy humanoid drivers.

AVs, if successful, will be a truly disruptive technology, changing not only the way we travel but the way we work, live and interact with one another. Many industries will be impacted by the implementation of AVs, with taxi and ride hailing companies like Uber utilising it directly whilst car manufacturers have been scrambling to adapt. As with AI, flurries of acquisitions have resulted from companies desperately trying to partner up and gain market share in what is already a hugely competitive field, but the rewards will be there. As of 2016, there were 30 companies already embedding AI into driverless cars, with Tesla, Google, and Apple the current heavyweights. As of March 2018, Apple has 45 self-driven cars on the streets. Waymo was spun off from Google into its own driverless car division and has racked up over 4 million self-driven miles as of November 2017. The rate at which these miles are accumulating are increasing exponentially; it took six years to reach the millionth mile but just a further 6 months to hit the fourth millionth. Uber is not too far behind either having clocked two million miles in December 2017. In an industry where data is king, this progress is rapid even by today's technological standard.

Multiple countries such as the UK and France are now allowing autonomous vehicles to be tested on public roads amongst their human counterparts, although most still require a human presence in the vehicle just in case emergency action is needed. It will be a long and bumpy road, however; even when the technology is there adoption will be curtailed by public perception and cost. Cars on the road today are of an average age of just over 11 years, so a full transition, if it were ever to occur, is always going to be gradual. And here the problem lies. Trying to programme computer algorithms to understand human rules of the road and human nuances such as why some drive within inches of another, others miles, why some allow cars to merge whilst others speed up to block them will be a huge hurdle to overcome. Will human drivers, upon seeing an autonomous vehicle, take advantage of the lack of consciousness and pull out of a junction knowing the computer will stop for it? All these questions and the many more we don't even know will need to be addressed, presenting an enormous challenge. Fortunately, it is well worth fighting for. The benefits are clear to see; shorter journey times, less pollution, perfect safety statistics and a more productive use of time will improve our lives to no end, turning that dreaded rush hour commute into a time where we can just sit back and relax.

Autonomous Vehicles

Electric Avenue

Autonomous vehicles have recently come of age due to the accumulation of decades of developments in software and hardware. Recent hardware innovations such as radar, odometry, lasers, and computer vision allow for a detailed computer perception of a vehicle's environment in a quick enough time frame for computer software programs to successfully react to, predict outcomes and take the appropriate measures. These environmental objects include other cars, pedestrians, relevant signage and navigation routes, all essential to navigating even the most basic of journeys.

Computer hardware in the past few decades has been hugely progressive, with the observation of Moore's law and the doubling of the number of transistors on a chip approximately every two years. This has allowed the development of measuring technologies such as LIDAR (light detection and ranging) resulting in the ability of a computer to calculate the distance of any visible object in a range of approximately 60 m with an accuracy of around 2cm. LIDAR, GPS, and other sensory tech are becoming progressively cheaper, more powerful and more reliable, opening up new possibilities such as self-driving vehicles. The ability to use this technology, however, relies on the software, which acts as a sort of middleman, translating the analogue world it senses into digital information the algorithm can recognise. Recent artificial intelligence (AI) developments such as machine learning and artificial neural networks have progressed the field significantly, transforming the old methods of sluggish brute force analysis (analysing every possible scenario) into more finely tuned continuous improvement learning, resulting in much quicker and more accurate outputs. Software is the key component for future progress, turning AVs from expensive specialised systems to commercial, flexible and reliable staples of everyday life.

The Society of Automotive Engineers (SAE) has devised a lexicon of autonomy to represent the progressive levels of autonomy (represented by levels 0-5):

Level 0 - All controls are manually operated (steering, braking, throttle). This is what all cars up to 1960 have been and how the majority are driven even today.

Level 1 - Specific single functions can be automated such as the throttle via cruise control and steering via lane assist, not both at the same time, however, this would be classed as level 2. Cruise control appeared on Cadillacs and Chryslers from around the 1960s. Although a specific function is automated, the vehicle is not, however, as a human must have control of the wheel or pedals at all times.

Level 2 - Specific functions such as those listed above can be combined to allow successful travel without a human touching the steering or pedals. Cruise control and lane assist ensures the vehicle travels autonomously without human interference but a human must always be alert and prepared to take control back at any moment. Whereas level 1 still requires human control, level 2 can be completely automated in some situations (motorway driving for example).

Level 3 - Here we shift it up a gear. In specific controlled environments vehicles are completely autonomous and can take the driver to their destination, without any input in operating controls, from start to finish. Although there is no human input necessarily, I still say driver because they must still be fully alert and able to take control at any point during the journey. Currently, these vehicles are being tested by the likes of Waymo and Uber and are on the cusp of becoming commercialised. The use of level 3 vehicles, however, is limited to certain traffic and environmental conditions within which they are allowed to operate.

Level 4 - This is where a vehicle can finally be called truly autonomous. No human driver is required as the vehicle is safe enough to conduct all phases of the journey without interference. The key difference (and increase in difficulty) is that the human needs not pay attention to the road and is free to read a book, talk on the phone or even have a snooze. It is still bound, however, by certain driving limits and must operate within its "operational design domain" (ODD). Waymo has chosen to jump directly into level 4 design, operating in specific parts of the city which are within the realms of control for the software.

Level 5 - Here we finally have a fully autonomous vehicle in every sense of the word and able to operate in all conditions. We are certainly a fair way off from this point but this is the end goal, at the point where autonomous vehicles become a utility; we simply enter our destination and think nothing more of it until we miraculously arrive. At this point, we are no longer driving, merely travelling like on a bus or a train.

We are currently on the brink of level 3. Audi's A8 is the first claimed level 3 vehicle, using its "Audi AI" to transport its occupants autonomously up to 60kph in certain conditions the software deems appropriate. There is a significant step between level 3 and 4, however; the software required to make this jump will take years of data collection and continuous improvement to reliably and safely manage the unpredictability that comes with town driving. The AI behind the systems has three main components; perception, planning, and control. Firstly, perception refers to the ability of the software to collect information from all available sources (sensors, GPS etc.). Perception is comprised of two subsections working in tandem; environmental perception creates an image of the vehicles surroundings such as objects, other cars, and road markings whilst localisation identifies where exactly the vehicle lies within this environment. Secondly, we have planning which allows the software to make informed decisions with the input data gathered from the perception stage. Finally, control refers to taking the appropriate solution once all perception and planning tasks have been completed. Perception and planning are the more difficult parts and require thorough software programs to best utilise the collected data inputs to create the most appropriate outputs.

As with most emerging technologies of late, data collection and its corresponding analysis and application will be the crucial parameter in effective implementation. Tesla claims all its cars have level 5 technologies built into all their cars and has been running it in shadow mode; the software does all the perception, planning and control tasks but doesn't actually execute the decisions. Although limited to some extent (it cannot learn from its mistakes if it doesn't make any) the amount of data collecting through its hundreds of thousands of cars operating in this mode is huge, especially once its new "affordable" model 3 finally hits full production. Many are dubious of Tesla's level 5 claim altogether.

Despite the axiom, knowledge is power; knowledge (in this case data) is, in fact, useless without the correct implementation. In order to ensure that AVs move safely and efficiently, we need to share this data with other AVs. Vehicle to vehicle (V2V) communication allows neighbouring AVs to communicate data with others to best plan future movements and will be essential to successfully coordinate all AVs seamlessly, safely and reliably. Telematics such as speed, acceleration, destination, and current location would allow other vehicles to be able to (as accurately as the technology allows) plan their moves having safely regarded all other vehicle movements. In theory, this could spell the end for traffic lights and stop signs as vehicles would be able to time their passing perfectly through other vehicles without even slowing down. If all works as it should, there would be no accidents, minimal traffic and less wasted time and fuel. All of the above, of course, only works if all vehicles are connected (such as an eventual full transition to autonomous cars) and any non-autonomous vehicles (such as current human drivers) will prevent such a system from working flawlessly.

Similarly to V2V communications, vehicle to infrastructure (V2I) communication would also improve efficiency. As you might expect, this covers the communication between vehicles and the infrastructure, such as traffic lights, stop signs, crosswalks, overhead signs etc. The continual saturation o connected devices, these days including even fridges and washing machines, connected to the Internet of Things (IoT) will see a synergy between vehicles and their surroundings. In 2012, computer scientists at the University of Texas, Austin, began developing smart intersections for autonomous vehicles. It uses clever software to divide the area of an intersection in grids, with an oncoming vehicle allotted a number of squares for which it will pass (predicting position using telematics obtained from the oncoming vehicle). As long as no squares on the grid overlap from other vehicles allotted squares, the vehicles will pass through seamlessly. This would also work for car parks allotting spaces on a first come first serve basis, sending that mother of all scourges of trying to find a parking space into antiquity. V2V and V2I will be key to safe implementation of AVs, but it will forever struggle with the unpredictability that is human drivers. Ironically the only real factor slowing the transition from a dirty, inefficient and unsafe present to a safe, flawless and beneficial future for mankind may be man itself.

The human factor is a significant stumbling point; slowing and possibly even halting progress altogether. The infinite decisions a human can take every second means predicting and reacting in time is near impossible for software, no matter how sophisticated. Ideally, this problem will be solved at the point where AVs are fully saturated into the market, possibly and most likely by government legislation and law banning the use of non- autonomous cars due to environmental, social and safety pressures. Since the successful adoption of AVs will be heavily influenced by safety statistics, simply merging AVs onto current roads alongside the public will be a PR nightmare for both car makers and governments. Instead, the only safe way forward I can predict is to segregate AVs and non-AVs, at least until the infrastructure needed to more successfully merge the two is tangible. The first step would be banning non-AV vehicles from busy city centres such as Los Angeles, New York, and London where pollution, congestion, and noise are already critically damaging. AVs will also be readily welcomed as new autonomous vehicles will increasingly tend to be electrified as they are cheaper and easier to run, maintain and produce with their fewer moving components, reducing the effects from exhaust fumes and noise whilst also turning wasted traveling time into more productive time. In a controlled environment such as a city centre where hedonistic humans cannot interfere with omniscient calculated software decisions, AVs can flourish and maximise their advantages. When combined with shared vehicles and ride hailing, the effects would be transformational for those who live and work within these AV operational areas.

What about outside these bordered utopias? Major and minor roads linking cities are vital for economic growth. Despite carrying 40% of road traffic, these more rural roads result in 60% of accidents (UK 2013, a similar trend observed elsewhere around the world). It is easier to merge autonomous and non-autonomous vehicles on motorways where it is mostly straight line driving for long periods of time. To utilise the higher speeds AVs could offer over non-AVs (no rubbernecking, driving closer together etc), separate lanes restricted to just AV use may eventually be added to highways similar to how HOV (high occupancy vehicle) lanes operate in North America. As "smart motorway" designs become increasingly more technologically capable, V2I communication will allow lanes to automatically adjust traffic flows depending on conditions, perhaps dedicating multiple lanes to AVs when conditions permit. Whatever the method, I can only foresee the segregation of AVs and non-AVs in the short term to ensure safety statistics surrounding AV adoption remains socially acceptable.

Ride Hailing

Reinventing the Wheel

Over the past century, personal cars have transformed from a novelty for the rich to a staple of most people's lives. It may seem strange to think now that the earliest horseless carriages were seen as a fad. Appearing around 1900 they were not seen in the same utilitarian fashion we know them today, more an expensive toy for the rich to inquire over. As with most nascent industries, vehicles became increasingly faster, reliable and cheaper, with the iconic Ford Model T in 1908 opening an entry point of car ownership to the masses. Freeing the middle class from the limitations of geography, Ford went from selling 1700 vehicles in 1904 to over 1 million by 1920, a boom that has continued to this very day. Cars have also become synonymous with affluence; Mr Jones' new Mercedes on the drive suggests to his neighbour that he must be doing very well, seemingly better than him and his 2008 Camry. He must, therefore, keep up, purchasing a new Lexus to remind Mr Jones that he too is doing well. And thus the cycle continues. After 100 years, this model of car ownership looks set to change, however, pulling a complete handbrake turn from private ownership to a sharing culture.

The incumbent car ownership model is now falling victim to its own success, however. The unbounded geographical movements unlocked by early cars have now resulted in massive city congestion. LA has been in the public spotlight recently with the average motorist spending 102 hours sitting idle in mind-numbing traffic at peak times every year, costing each an eye-watering $2408 in wasted fuel and productivity. An extreme example but it highlights the fact that the convenience offered by vehicles has outpaced its dependant infrastructural needs, now resulting in environmental and social movements against them. The resulting higher costs mentioned, combined with rising insurance, vehicle tax, and congestion charges and increasing city rents have pushed many younger career driven millennials to seek the convenience of a new travel model opened by the likes of Uber, Lyft and Sidecar to name just a few. The combination of ride hailing and autonomy, together with the cleanliness and efficiency of electric vehicles, provides an increasingly viable alternative model of transport, undermining the logic of car ownership for many city goers.

Ride hailing is one of those evolutionary innovations that solve a problem through the beauty of simplicity. Similar to how the iPhone combined a phone, music player and internet browser into one portable device, autonomous ride hailing will simplify the complexities of owning, maintaining and paying for a vehicle to a simple, cheap and convenient pay per use model. Simply open the relevant app on your smartphone, input a destination and some other essential criteria, hop in and wait until you arrive, doing whatever (within reason) you wish during the journey. Forget the annual battle with your insurance company over why your premium has increased through no fault of your own, forget taxing your car, congestion charges, paying for parking, forget getting your car dinged by an irritating little juvenile who seemingly develop superhuman strength when opening car doors. All you pay is a set price per distance while all the difficult and technical details are done for you behind the scenes.

Traditional taxis have always typically cost more than private vehicles when considering the total cost per mile, and despite ride hailing firms generally pushing the price of hailed journeys down a little, they are still more expensive than the traditional car ownership model. The current cost for ride hailing in the rich world is an average of $2.50 per mile compared to $1.20 for owning and operating a private car. UBS, a banking firm, estimates that the driver comprises 60% of this cost for ride hailing. Automation will obviously eliminate this driver cost and, when combined with electrification and competition, predicts the cost per mile to drop to $0.70 per mile. This presents a significant saving, enough to surely tempt most drivers to cede control to machines. At this rate, a typical household driving an average of 10,000 miles a year could save $5,000.

Despite ride hailing currently costing double the price per mile compared to owning a private vehicle, Uber's 8 million users across 83 countries and 674 cities deem this difference a price worth paying, resulting in 40 million monthly rides whilst also showing the increasing influence and use of ride hailing services. This is only expected to increase; UBS also expect 80% of city travellers to use robotaxis by 2035. Even more boldly, they claim by 2030 a quarter of passenger miles in the US will be in shared self-driving electric vehicles resulting in 60% fewer cars on city streets, 80% less emissions and 90% less accidents. It is those last two points of reducing emissions and accidents that governments will look to take advantage of to push through autonomous vehicle legislation.

Although ride hailing apps have grabbed a lot of the spotlight, it is more specifically ride sharing that will unlock the path towards efficiency. Ride sharing is a further development in the current movement of the "sharing economy", a now ubiquitous term for an economic system in which goods and services are shared between private individuals, usually for a fee, with companies such as Airbnb, Parkatmyhouse and Lyft making use of unused rooms, parking or cars in order to maximise efficiency and profit for the renter. 20% of Uber's users opt for the sharing sub service UberPOOL, a service that lets you decide whether you want to share your ride or not. For those who do not mind sharing a ride, the price of their journey could be reduced from $12 for a private ride to $8 or so for a shared one. I personally do not mind sharing, especially for short journeys or commutes where it does not differ much to a bus or train in terms of social interaction but avoids the pitfalls of buses such as fixed inflexible routes, dirty and loud, taking up lots of space and blocking other vehicles whenever they stop. Still, many people will never want to share, and that's fine as long as they have the resources and ability to pay for their own vehicle as most of us in the rich world do. Our view is skewed, however, as we are among the 5% of people in the world who earn over an equivalent of $15000 a year. For everyone else who cannot afford the luxury of private travel, ride sharing opens an era of mass mobilisation and efficiency, a key for increasing productivity and GDP.

Whereas a car today needs to be stylish, cool and aesthetic, a shared or hailed autonomous vehicle does not as it is merely in use for the duration of one trip. We don't care what a taxi looks like, only that is clean, cheap and safe. This change in user needs mean hailed and shared vehicles in the future could cater more to internal luxuries such as comfortable seating, televisions (and the inevitable intrusion of advertisements), perhaps even beds for longer journeys with the price for such luxuries adjusting to suit. As the mechanicals of these pods can simply be bought from their corresponding manufacturers, opportunities may open for other non-automotive companies to design their own pods and interiors in a bid to gain market share.

The societal effects autonomous ride hailing and sharing services may bring could be a double-edged sword; there is much to gain from successful implementation but doing so whilst avoiding the plethora of potential pitfalls will require careful and thoughtful planning, implementation and regulation. Autonomous taxis and shared vehicles could operate non stop (excluding servicing and charging times) avoiding cars sitting idle unproductively for the 95% of the time that personal vehicles, on average, are unused. An MIT study cites research from the University of Texas, claiming that AVs acting as a taxi or shared car could replace up to nine individually operated vehicles. It could, therefore, be concluded that fewer cars result in less traffic. There are reasons to counter this common claim, however. The convenience afforded by motoring has resulted in the near-inevitable side effect of large and rapid urban growth. Living in close proximity to others allows for convenient access to restaurants, shops, friends and business connections, promoting opportunities and efficiencies for those who live there. These conveniences raise property prices as more and more people are lured to this beneficial living arrangement. At some point, the growth outpaces vital resources such as housing and road infrastructure and soon leads to overcrowding - an equilibrium point where costs outstrip benefits and the rate of growth declines.

This same equilibrium point applies to transport too. As a new road is built or upgraded, and the traffic capacity increases, it will indeed ease congestion in the surrounding areas, but research suggests this effect inevitably proves temporary. Nowhere is this clearer than the New York subway when it was extended into north Manhattan. The new route enabled commuters to live further away from the dirty and expensive city whilst still benefiting from the business and societal advantages offered from the proximate city life. Hence the city grew until growth was again limited by the travelling capacity as is the present situation, with the current state of the subway in dire need of investment to the tune of over $100 bn.

This effect is informally dubbed the fundamental law of road congestion; traffic easing after a capacity upgrade proves temporary as the newly created space proves beneficial for new residents and transport intensive economic activity. This benefit dies off as more and more people utilise the extra capacity until a point where the negatives of congestion and the positives of productivity reach a limiting equilibrium point. It would, therefore, be wasteful to try to achieve uncongested roads at a point below the equilibrium level as this would lessen the return on investment for the road project and result in underutilisation for business activity, both wasteful. Above the magic ratio, however, would also result in economic waste as congestion and traffic stifles movement and productivity. The highest efficiencies will come by being right on the equilibrium point (and of course this is where the difficulty lies for planners). The mass adoption of ride hailing and sharing services, therefore, may not result in a significant reduction in traffic and congestion as is so commonly thought, in fact the convenience and ease of taking a hailed vehicle may entice more users to make trips, most likely increasing the total number of trips but certainly increasing the number of miles travelled. Other advances previously mentioned such as V2V and V2I communications may help to reduce congestion by increasing mobility but the most direct method of controlling congestion will be via policy pricing.

The manic growth of automobiles over the past century has far outpaced its infrastructural needs, with many roads hurriedly constructed, sometimes without the necessary data or planning to reliably estimate future flows, resulting in reworks and widening works occurring years later than they should have and traffic management a seemingly constant firefighting exercise. This rapid growth did not afford planners and governments the time to adequately price the usage of the scarce resource of roads, resulting in congestion and overcrowding as users fight each other for its use. In the UK and other similar countries, use of the road is essentially free. The roads are paid for and maintained by national and local taxes (not "road tax" which doesn't exist and was abolished in 1939), but we are free to use them as little or often as wanted.

Road pricing has been gaining more and more traction amongst policy planners, with the idea that a price per mile method of payment should be introduced for road users based on the vehicle and its use. Although controversial, it may be the only viable way to fund infrastructure demands which are desperately needed to meet demand.

V2V and V2I in conjunction with other technologies allow AVs to be tracked and a picture of traffic and its flows to be gathered. Information from the masses of vehicles can allow planners to see which roads are the most congested, the most used, the least utilised or which roads have the most blockages or potholes and what times the worst congestion occurs. Sensors could even determine which areas are the most polluted or result in the most noise. The possibilities are plentiful and data collected would be infinitely useful for government planners to price usage of the road. Similar to congestion charges in London, the most congested areas are accordingly priced higher to limit the number of vehicles passing through, reducing congestion and raising revenue from those users who value the road space the most. Live data feeds from vehicles would improve upon this tremendously as pricing policies would be flexible and based not upon generalisations like the London congestion charge but on current actual conditions. Tolls and charges favour use of the road by those who value it the most, resulting in the most efficient use of that space, whose efficiencies will then be passed on to the consumer through pricing a journey per mile. Journeys will be priced by a finely tuned algorithm using the masses of live input data from the network of AVs and outputting appropriate routes with their corresponding price per mile based on data such as time of day, traffic levels, number of sharers etc.

I can feel you balking in your chair already, why would you want to pay for something like road use which you once received for free? It would be a painful transition but it will be made substantially easier by autonomous ride hailing and sharing services which are already priced per mile, similar to taxis which have acceptably had the same pricing policy for decades. Careful pricing of roads, however, creates a fairer system for maintaining the road infrastructure; lorries and heavy vehicles which do considerably more damage and create more pollution will rightly have to pay more than the occasional Sunday driver.

This will not only increase revenues but make those who benefit more from using the road pay more for its upkeep, thus reducing the burden on those who use it less. Careful pricing will also decrease road wear and congestion by increasing the fare rate for those roads more susceptible to damage and hence discouraging algorithms from using it as much. Co-founder and current president of Lyft, John Zimmer, thinks that in a few years road users will be subscribing to a miles plan similar to the way you do for data on a mobile phone contract. Although the idea of paying per mile may seem miserable, especially for those who regularly clock up the miles, the gained efficiencies combined with heavy competition should result in a better deal for most people. On a nationwide scale, it will benefit infrastructure budgets hugely, assuming the revenues are adequately managed and applied.

Adoption

You'll Never Catch me in one of Those

As with most disruptive technologies, there are large hurdles to overcome and problems to solve to prove the viability and reliability of autonomous vehicles. Safety is the most vocal of issues as society deals with a handover of control to systems beyond their physical control. A survey by the Governors Highway Safety Association finds that 56% of Americans still say no to riding in an autonomous vehicle, with 24% not trusting the technology and 22% stating safety concerns. To set the scene, global annual fatalities for vehicles total 1.3 million with a further 20-50 million injured or disabled. This averages 3287 a day or a death every 30 seconds. The loss both emotionally and economically to the state is a colossal waste and often overlooked. Human error is estimated to be the cause of 94% - 96% percent of all incidents, showing the potential improvement available from reducing this human factor.

Due to the overwhelming number of fatalities, the unfortunate souls who lose their lives often go unnoticed by the masses, yet a recent death of a pedestrian by an autonomous vehicle grabbed global attention. On March 18th, 2018, Uber reported their first death from an autonomous vehicle in Tempe,

Arizona. It appeared a pedestrian crossed the road (not on a designated crosswalk) and the AV failed to stop. A human driver was present in the car and still failed to notice the pedestrian, apparently checking the computer systems and not looking at the road. A couple of fatalities have also been blamed on Tesla's Autopilot system; the first on January 20th, 2016 in China and the second on May 7th, 2016 from a crash with an 18-wheeler. This makes 3 known fatalities due to self-driving cars, but whereas Tesla's level 2 autopilot doesn't claim to be fully autonomous (it requires a human to be able to intervene at any moment) Uber's fatality drew so much attention because it was a level 3 capable vehicle and aiming to complete all aspects of the journey without the need for human interference. It was also the first time a third party victim was involved, introducing ethical concerns.

Unfortunately, safety statistics cannot be reliably drawn for autonomous vehicles due to the small sample size of autonomous vehicle-related fatalities. Elon Musk tweeted with his usual bluster of bravado about the safety statistics of his autopilot system with just one death in 130 million AVMT (autonomous vehicle miles travelled) which is indeed better than the US average of 94 million VMT for human drivers. Having just passed 222 million miles and with the two recorded deaths mentioned above the average is now 111 million AVMT, still above the average but very susceptible to further decline. Just one more death will result in one death per 74 million and a further death will drop the average to 56 million AVMT. With Tesla's two recorded fatalities occurring within just over 3 months of each in 2016, the statistics are susceptible to rapid decrease and thus unreliable and fairly unhelpful. Only time and a growing mileage average will determine if AVs are indeed safer than their human counterpart but there is no doubt, whether justified or not, that any AV-related fatality will draw huge attention and potentially set progress back greatly.

Waymo is also building up its mileage, now at over 4 million miles (although in a more controlled environment), and the few incidents it has experienced have been reported to be the fault of the other (human) driver involved. Despite these promising statistics, adoption by the masses will require AVs to be (perhaps unjustifiably) almost completely infallible, certainly many multiples safer than the currently accepted human drivers. The safer they become the more difficult it becomes to make progress; a safety rating of 99%, for example, may be possible within 5 - 10 years. 100%, however, may take decades and the costs required to improve this 1% would almost certainly outweigh any profit, thus reducing investments and stifling progress.

Other safety concerns involve the typical ethical decisions a computer would have to make, such as whether the algorithm would make a decision to kill the single driver in order to avoid killing multiple pedestrians. Situations like this are popular because they draw upon the emotional aspect of AI systems but in reality, they are very situational, unlikely and therefore fairly irrelevant. The usual reaction to almost every accident is to slam on the brakes, rarely is there time or distance to manoeuvre or change course during the very short time between identifying a potential incident and the collision itself, rendering this question situational and fairly irrelevant. Others fear of a hijacking of the car's systems. Failsafe systems such as a manual stop system from inside the car could prevent this, however, and increasingly sophisticated encryption protocols will also help prevent these sorts of crimes from occurring. Automated car bombs are also a concern for some, but I can't see how it will be any easier for a terrorist to hack a hugely secure server system than it is to manually drive a vehicle into pedestrians as we have unfortunately witnessed in London and New York over the past few years. I am not denying the possibilities of any of these concerns, just stating their relative improbability and how few and far between situational incidents like these would be on a large scale.

Surprisingly (or perhaps not so) the survey also found consumer's wallets just as influential of a factor as safety for the adoption of AVs. A survey by J.D. Power and Associates found 37% of those who initially expressed interest in purchasing AVs later dropped to 20% once told that the extra technology would cost $3000 or more than a non- automated vehicle. With the average US transaction price of a new car or truck being $33,500, a 9% rise in car costs was enough to dissuade 45% of those interested from purchasing an autonomous vehicle, highlighting the highly inelastic response to car pricing. This also works in reverse, however. Another survey found that 75% of its participants would consider buying an AV, increasing to 86% when told their insurance would be cheaper. As a side note, 32% said they would not continue to drive once autonomous vehicles were available instead.

There are many other barriers to adoption, such as the influence automotive lobbyists exert on government policy and legislation, with automotive manufacturing a powerful tool for negotiating governments and job protection a key issue for Donald Trump's protectionist America. As much as governments relish the power they hold from a strong automotive industry, they would doubly hate to lose this to the increasingly worrying monopolies such as Google and Amazon, whose sheer size and power are starting to worry more populist outlooks. But perhaps the biggest stumbling point will be freedom; since man first sat behind the wheel of a vehicle the connection between man and machine has been a love affair that has created multi-billion dollar passions from classic cars to Formula 1. There is very little that compares with the adrenaline rush of speed or the thrill of driving antique vehicles, something, I included, would never want to give up. What will happen to private cars? Will they be banned or kept to specific areas? This would be a red flag for many drivers. Combining this with the collection of people's data and potential intrusion of advertisements into ride hailing services, the lack of freedom afforded to us today seems overwhelming to many.

Chapter Summary

Throughout this chapter, we have seen many of the potential benefits afforded by the introduction of autonomous vehicles. We can expect cheaper travel, safer roads, less congestion, less idle traffic, faster journey times, cleaner cities and fewer city areas wasted housing vehicles which remain unused for 95% of the time. These conveniences will open up the path for autonomous ride hailing and shared vehicles, which takes the current stressful car ownership model and reduces it with a beautifully simply price per mile policy which looks set to become cheaper per mile than that of private personal vehicles. Simply hail a ride on your phone, select your criteria (shared users, arrival time, level of extras wanted etc.) and pay per mile. Contract options will more than likely surface with users paying a monthly fee for a set number of monthly miles such as that of cellular minutes and data. The first wave of autonomous vehicles may be restricted to confined city perimeters as governments and local councils are forced to take action against destructive levels of congestion, pollution, and noise by replacing them with safe, efficient and quiet electric autonomous vehicles.

Successful implementation will depend on government policy and legislation, with congestion and urban sprawl potential increasing as AVs increased conveniences entice more people to make journeys. Current planning and policy-making, however, will create a fairer system of paying for the maintenance of the roads, with those who use and damage it the most paying more for its upkeep. The mix of human and AV vehicles, however, will be difficult and despite the thousands of deaths occurring due to human drivers each year, every single autonomous vehicle-related death will draw much attention and criticism, unfairly stifling progress. Safety and cost concerns are the largest obstacles to mass adoption; until the costs are clearly beneficial to consumers, uptake will remain gradual as it is today. A lack of freedom and privacy is also a justifiable worry, with many unwilling to cede complete control to a machine and some unwilling to try altogether. There is someone who has already overcome all of these public opinion concerns already, however, as Henry Ford once quipped: "If I had asked people what they wanted, they would have said faster horses".

5. Energy

Power to the People

Whilst all the aforementioned technologies are primed to improve mankind's quality of life, they all depend on one key ingredient. Energy. Despite the daily barrage of news articles regarding terrorism and poor economic health, none are globally more important than the energy crisis we will one day face. In fact, many issues, whether political or economic (much the same thing) stem from an issue of energy; in a fossil-fuel world, control over oil and gas reserves is an essential component of national power. There will come a time where the status quo of fossil-fuel maintained power will cease to be stable, either through supply levels or environmental, social and economic issues.

Almost everything society relies on daily, from smartphones and computers to the hot cup of coffee you may well be enjoying right now, is a result of energy advancements. Your brand new fancy phone may have an impressive 6GB RAM with a 6.3-inch quad HD+ AMOLED HDR display but without energy to charge it, it may as well be a brick. Desalination of seawater has been technically possible since the development of the first land-based desalination plant in 1928, yet 1 in 9 people globally still don't have access to clean water close to home. Diarrhoea caused by a lack of access to clean water kills a child every 2 minutes. Despite the technical know-how to convert seawater to freshwater, energy limits the technology from reaching those desperately in need. Due to the very high energy demands of the desalination process, the resulting cost of water produced is approximately 10 times higher than collecting spring water. This will hopefully one day be overcome with further technology advances, but this is just one of a whole host of reasons why the world will become increasingly more dependant on energy developments.

Energy is what drives economic growth and is frequently referred to as the "oxygen of the economy." Yet economic growth further drives energy demands, of which we can only meet through continual use of unsustainable technology such as coal, oil, and gas. With India and Africa yet to fully develop a compressive energy network like that of developed countries, the quantity of future energy required to fulfil this growth is colossal.

According to the latest data from the Internal Energy Agency (IEA 2018), the world's demand for energy grew by 2.1% in 2017, more than twice that of 2017. 40% of this growth was attributed to strong economic growth in China and India, of which 72% was met by coal, oil, and gas. Renewables contributed an impressive 25% and the rest by nuclear. Electricity generation demands were greater than energy demands at 3.1% (electricity is only part of total energy demands, the rest comprises of transportation, heating etc.), once again mostly from China and India.

This increase in demand, however, has been satisfied by the only way we know how; fossil fuels. According to data from the CIA Fact book, demand for coal, the dirtiest and least efficient fuel of all, grew by 1%, reversing the previous two years' downward trend, due in large part to new coal-fired plants in Asia. Although the much cleaner and more efficient nuclear power generation grew by 3%, the net capacity added after decommissioned nuclear plants barely grew. Despite renewables meeting an impressive 25% of global energy growth, the resulting dominance in fossil fuel capacity has taken a toll on global energy-related CO_2 emissions, growing by 1.4% after 3 years of flat growth.

Although climate change through the excessive burning of fossil fuels is now generally accepted, the impending permanent damage from our current trajectory is still widely underestimated. The devastating wildfires in Greece which has claimed 74 lives and thousands of buildings, and in California, where 10 have died and a colossal 688,000 acres of land has been burned, is merely the beginning of a worrying trend. The excessive heat waves experienced around the world in the summer of 2018 are also suspected consequences of global warming, where a one-degree rise in global temperature makes such extremes in temperature more likely. Warmer ocean waters have also pushed the jet stream further north and have trapped high-pressure systems leading to longer lasting heat waves. Such one in a thousand events is now much more likely and this sort of extreme weather can be expected to become both more severe and frequent.

Environmental consequences aside, the issue of supply is also an inevitable concern. Formed over 300 million years, the technological progress made since the industrial revolution has seen man use a significant amount of these finite fuels in just 200 years. Accounting for current trends, crude oil reserves are depleting at 4bn tonnes a year, eliminating our known reserves by 2052. The elimination of crude oil will put further demand on gas, of which our supplies are then estimated to last until 2060. From here it is coal which will be relied on, which, despite having large reserves, is expected to last until 2088. Not that we would be able to live in a world where that quantity of filthy material is burned to that extreme. Coal is amongst the easiest and cheapest forms of energy; in the event of a global blackout, perhaps due to extreme weather or war, coal is a reassuring resource to have stockpiled to ensure civilization can function to some degree. Without this safety net, global politics will be much higher stakes.

Renewables

Will Renewables get the Green Light?

It may not come as much of a surprise to learn that installation of renewable energy has been increasing year after year for the past decade or so. Without bombarding you with too many statistics, the new energy capacity installed from renewable sources in 2016 was between 139-161GW, depending on the study. This represents an 8-10% rise in 2015 and sets a new record for renewable penetration. Another record was for the proportion of new electricity generation capacity from renewables (out of a total installed) at 55% for the year 2016. As a result, renewable global power capacity stands at 17% (up 2% from 2015) and electricity generation at 11.3% (up 1% from 2015). The difference between capacity and generation comes from the capacity factor of the energy source, i.e. the difference between the average realised electrical output of the source compared to the maximum possible output per time period. At the top end of this scale stands nuclear power at 90% (very efficient), moving down to coal at 64%, gas at 43%, and solar at 34%. These values are all averaged and taken from the US.

One might think that this yearly increase in renewable capacity is a sure-fire indicator of the health of renewables and its inevitable position as the top clean and cheap zero carbon power source. There are concerns, however. This record capacity required an investment of $242bn, 23% less than that invested 2015. A positive reason for the higher capacity despite a lower investment is mainly due to the decrease in cost per megawatt of renewables (i.e. more power can be obtained for less money). In dollar terms, this cost decreased by 10% for solar and wind representing the lowering costs of the underlying technology. Incidentally, this investment was also larger than that of fossil fuel investment by nearly double. Investors are therefore getting more bang for their buck, a promising sign for future uptake. Another, rather less positive, cause for the drop in investment comes from a huge decrease in investment from many countries, with China and Japan contributing a large part of this share. Whether this decrease in investment is a temporary blip or the start of a trend is yet to be seen, but one can confidently assume that the use of renewable energy sources will rise in future years.

Renewables have become so important for reasons far beyond the environment. Jobs associated with renewable energy are estimated to be near 7.7m globally, with solar photovoltaics (PV, i.e. solar panels) contributing the bulk of this. The fact that renewable energy costs are now competitive with fossil fuels has fuelled this rapidly growing multibillion-dollar industry, resulting in lots of competition within the sector. This competition has driven innovation and efficiency, and thus the cycle of innovation continues. In the US alone, renewable energy jobs outnumber jobs from fossil fuels by a factor of 2.5, despite Donald Trump doing his utmost to prevent the inevitable demise of fossil fuels as a primary source.

Mr Trump segues us to perhaps the most important reason for the inevitable rise of renewables; the fragile environment. Despite various tweets affirming his scepticism in man-made global warming, and announcing his intention to pull America out of the Paris Climate Accord (an agreement between 196 members to limit the global average temperature rise to below 2º), one simply cannot reasonably deny the need to limit global warming and preserve the planet before it becomes irreparable. Dealing with the damage to the environment is similar to maintaining a car. Taking a "I'll change it next week" approach to engine oil, for example, may save you $50 today, but could end up costing you thousands when your engine seizes up. A similar occurrence is happening with our environment, although the environment cannot simply be replaced.

A significant part of the problem lies in basic human psychology, as one social experiment highlights particularly well. Three people had one minute to decide between them who should get a free $100, all they needed to do was unanimously agree a name. Seeing as the money was completely free and they had absolutely nothing to lose and just needed to say a name, they failed to come to any conclusion and the money was lost. The fear of them "losing" $100 despite not having it in the first place was enough to sabotage the whole group and ensure no one got anything. This inherent flaw of natural human greed also rears its ugly head when it comes to climate change. People are too focused on the short-term gain (particularly politicians who can be too easily influenced by lobbyists and whose only concern is the short duration of their elected terms) to see the bigger picture. Although an extreme example, one cannot be blamed for this hereditary faux pas. I am certainly not free from guilt; I drive a dirty polluting diesel because it gets good miles per gallon and saves me money. The only way to overcome this problem is for penalties to be put in place which would cost me more (a new tax on diesel cars for example), which, if steep enough, would make it cheaper for me to run an electric car. For the environment this would take the form of a carbon tax where companies are taxed based on how much CO_2 they release, with the money raised used to offset rising temperature levels and companies, now financially incentivised, will either release fewer CO_2s or pay more for higher emissions. This would be complicated and difficult to fairly implement as some industries are naturally more polluting than others but will be essential for taking responsibility for emissions. Obama had great difficulty pushing through a carbon tax during his term and now Trump is president, the chances are very slim indeed. The good news is, even without a carbon tax, renewables are now mature enough that when the inevitable tax does come to fruition, renewables (especially solar) will gain momentum tremendously as it is already a very viable option with significant amounts of research and development already achieved.

So what forms of renewable energy will we be seeing in the not too distant future? It depends largely on where you are. Whereas dispatchable energy (energy sources that can be turned on or off at will) such as gas and coal can be situated almost anywhere, non-dispatchable energy (most renewable sources) is at the mercy of the environment. No sun, no solar generation, no wind, no wind power. Locations on islands or exposed to miles of coastland are excellently suited to wind farms and have seen large surges of investment over the last decade. Denmark is the current pioneer of wind energy which now produces 42% of its total electricity consumption, and the wind alone has, on occasion, produced a surplus of energy. Wind farms can also be very space efficient, as they make use of vertical space. Many wind farms are also combined with agricultural activity where the land in between the turbines can be farmed, creating very efficient use of land. Onshore wind farms are also relatively inexpensive, proving just slightly more expensive than coal per MW (not accounting for environmental impacts, however). Offshore farms such as those far out in the ocean, however, can harvest much more energy as offshore winds can be on average 90% stronger than that on land. Offshore farms have much higher costs, however, (roughly double) and are much more complicated to integrate into a grid, but do alleviate aesthetic concerns that land-based turbines attract.

Solar power will certainly continue to gather steam and will almost certainly become the dominant source of renewable power. Two forms of solar power currently show huge promise and are relatively mature: photovoltaics (PV, i.e. solar panels) and CSP (concentrated solar power). As of 2014, an estimated 90% of installed solar power in the US consisted of PV installations, currently dominating the solar scene. In a similar manner to how computer chips double in computing power every 2 years, research and development into photovoltaics have seen similar progress. Few industries have seen their growth accelerate in the way the PV industry has, with incentives such as America's Million Solar Roofs programme and the inclusion of renewables within China's five-year plan for energy production creating an environment where solar panels are commercially viable, opening the technology to competition and thus innovation and price reduction.

Despite the ever-increasing popularity of domestic solar supplied such as rooftop solar power, and companies such as Tesla introducing solar roof tiles, it is the utility side of solar power which is likely to dominate due to the economies of scale that solar farms provide. The estimated cost per peak watt for a residential PV system is 80% greater than that of utility scale. To understand why, it is important to understand the two main costs associated with PV panels. The first is the module cost which comes from the physical internal components of the panels. Like most technology, this has been decreasing as research and development progresses. This module cost is the same for both residential and utility as the components are mostly the same. The cost variance between residential and utility PV panels, therefore, is a result of the second factor, known as the balance of system effects (BOS). This represents all other components such as wiring, brackets, inverters etc. As module costs have kept decreasing, BOS costs now represent 85% of the cost for a residential system as opposed to 65% for utility scale. This is primarily due to the benefits of economies of scale mentioned earlier. For the consumer, residential scale average price per peak Watt stands at $4.90, compared to just $1.80 for utility systems. A lot of this price difference is the result of the structure of the residential PV market, where the complexity of installation, subsidies and government structure for different areas creates inefficiencies. Ultimately, however, it will be the price the consumer pays that limits or accelerates the uptake of solar power, the main reason why utility scale farms are dominating investment.

Most, if not all, environmentalists the world over would long strive to see the day that renewable energy powers 100% of all energy demands, eliminating all damage associated with dirty fuels and creating a clean utopia seen in most sci-fi films. This, however, is not practicable and will almost certainly never happen (despite probably being technically possible). Once again the reason is economical. Non-dispatchable renewable energy (it cannot be turned on or off at will) is highly intermittent. Despite claims from fantastical statistics, such as Europe having 30,000TWh of onshore and offshore energy potential annually, enough to power itself ten times over, or the US having an estimated 400,000TWh of annual potential solar power, enough to power itself 100 times over, statements like these are based on average annual renewable productions, which although theoretically correct, would not work in application. The intermittency of renewable energy (particularly solar and wind) is the fundamental problem, meaning the actual output is highly unpredictable and variable.

Take solar power, for example (the following data was obtained from the MIT Energy Initiative). Unsurprisingly, solar peaks in the middle of the day and in summer. When the sun is 60° above the horizon, the sun's intensity is still 87% of its maximum (when shining on a horizontal surface). Drop down to an angle of 15%, however, and the intensity quickly drops to just 25%. Looking more seasonally, a light cloud cover will produce a solar output of approximately 80%, whereas a heavy overcast day will drop that to a mere 15%. This is not such a large problem for highly insulated (exposed to the suns rays) locations such as California but has a profound effect on the viability of solar power in other areas. Even in the UK, which is seen as moderately suitable for solar power, a solar panel will produce 10 times less energy in December than in June. This increases to a whopping 65 times when comparing a sunny day in June to an overcast day in December. This poses an enormous, if not practically insurmountable, problem for energy planners.

There are a few solutions to overcome this issue, some more feasible than others. Firstly, the renewable energy capacity could be overscaled to satisfy the worst case scenario. In a scenario with 80% of electricity generated from renewables, six times more capacity than peak load is estimated to be needed in order to overcome the intermittency issue and ensure a continuous supply is available at all times. Ramping this up to 100% renewable energy and the overscaling would have to increase to ten times peak load, equating to more than the total EU annual electricity consumption. Physically this means ten times the number of solar and wind farms would be needed to overcome the issue of intermittency. Obvious economic implications aside, the environmental impact when considering the whole life cycle of building and maintaining the extra infrastructure needed to achieve this overscaling is more than likely to be greater than current CO_2 emissions from today's power grid. Essentially, the energy used in the full cycle of a power network with a high proportion of renewables would use more energy (and hence CO_2) than it saves. Compounding this effect is the relatively short lifespan of solar panels at an average of 20 years, roughly half that of coal and gas plants. PV panels are still in their developmental infancy when compared to the more mature fossil fuels and the rapid advancement in materials and technology quickly outdates the panels rendering them quickly redundant, similar to how the effects of Moore's Law ensures computers and phones are replaced every couple of years. This results in more energy and cost to regularly replace these panels as they become outdated.

A second option would be to utilise a large interconnected transmission network to exploit geographical areas which produce a consistent and larger amount of energy and distribute this excess energy across different regions. This smoothing effect would reduce the need to overscale the energy capacity by such a large margin by exploiting more reliable weather patterns from consistent geographies. This would also make the renewable equipment themselves more efficient as the utilisation rates (how often solar panels are actually converting energy) would be higher. Excess wind energy could be exported during blustery Scandinavian winters to other geographic areas who have less. Similarly, solar power during hot Spanish summers can be exported to places where the sun is more intermittent. A great advantage of this would be a more promising investment for building new renewable sources as any excess electricity would be sold and distributed somewhere else, increasing profit and minimising waste. This idea works better in more connected regions such as the EU where border movements of commodities and services are more fluid than those of more tense regions such as the Middle East. Again, the main issue occurs in the full CO_2 life cycle analysis of building and maintaining a vast cross-border supergrid which, even though reduced by resource smoothing, would still have to be overscaled to overcome intermittency issues. It could also be used as political leverage. New transmission lines are also unsightly and expensive, creating a bureaucratic nightmare for governments and resulting in approval periods of up to a decade.

Thirdly, we could store any surplus energy resulting from strong periods of renewable energy production and draw upon these reserves at peak times or when renewable production is low. The most promising method of energy storage is currently from batteries, specifically lithium-ion. Batteries over the past decades have made a steady slog of improvements with the price of a set capacity dropping by half approximately every 5-7 years. Although there are currently many different forms of new battery technology on the horizon, the recent success and adoption of ranged electric vehicles has only really become a commercial possibility within the last few years due to lithium-ion battery improvements. The fact that Elon Musk and his electric car company, Tesla, has invested an eye-watering $5 billion into the "Gigafactory", a purpose-built 5.5m sq. ft factory set to produce enough batteries for 1.5 million cars a year, hints at lithium ion being the most likely type of battery for commercial renewable storage in the foreseeable future. This is certainly promising for renewable energy uptake, but in reality, the full-scale adoption of batteries is stifled once again by the usual two culprits, cost and CO_2 emissions. As an example, the total solar capacity of the UK in 2008 was 460 TWh. Storing this capacity using lithium-ion batteries (and taking into account a charging/discharging efficiency of 85%) would require 644 million terajoules of primary energy (i.e. energy to manufacture the batteries), roughly equal to 15 times the annual primary energy used in the whole of Europe. The aforementioned life cycle of lithium-ion batteries also means this colossal energy input would have to be repeated every 20 years as battery technology becomes redundant, unfortunately rendering battery use for renewable storage (at this point in time) impractical.

Alas, all is not lost. The fourth solution would be to hybridise renewable sources with current dispatchable plants such as gas, coal, oil and nuclear. This will very much displease the die-hard greens who seek a 100% renewable future, but currently offers the only real, practical and tangible method to cut CO_2 emissions. Mixing renewable with dispatchable plants would allow for all renewable energy generated to be utilised, with the remaining energy needed to be provided by dispatchable power plants already in use. Although this defeats the purpose of switching away from fossil fuels towards clean sources, it is the most feasible way to wean ourselves of our mass reliance on fossil fuels whilst also encouraging the growth of renewables. Investment in renewable sources would likely be encouraged as all power generated could be sold (unlike standalone plants where energy production may have to be curtailed due to the overscaling issue mentioned earlier) and as renewable plants become more economically profitable in relation to fossil fuels, the penetration of renewables into mainstream energy generation will keep increasing. How far we could keep raising this limit will be limited by the cost and CO_2 input of building this new infrastructure vs. the saving we obtain from reducing the CO_2 from burning fossil fuels. What this percentage mix would be is very difficult to calculate and would depend on many factors such as if battery storage is used, type of renewable plant etc.

Natural gas plants would be the best place to start. Current global electricity production is dominated by coal plants at 40% followed by natural gas at 23%. Since natural gas releases a smidge over half the amount of CO_2 for the amount of released energy as coal, building new gas plants instead of coal plants would have an immediate positive impact in CO_2 level reductions. This would also be the most cost-effective way to introduce more renewable sources as the gas plants already planned or in commission can still live out their 40-year life cycle whilst ensuring continuity of energy and avoiding intermittency.

Long-term, however, the use of gas still presents a problem; it pollutes and is finite in quantity. A more sustainable long-term mix, therefore, would be a combination of renewable and nuclear power. This low CO_2 hybrid mix would help keep the climate temperature rise below the 2° target of the Paris agreement whilst also providing enough electricity for a likely increase in future demand. With new technology comes new demands; electric vehicles (cars, buses, planes, trains, ships) will only become more popular, with a very good chance of becoming the dominant transportation technology due to the advantages they offer over internal combustion engines, primarily being 80-90% efficient to combustion's 20-30%, full torque from stationary, much quieter with less moving parts and therefore cheaper maintenance.

With many countries currently proposing legislation to ban all fossil-fuelled cars by around 2040, the increase in energy demands will significantly increase when everyone charges their new electric car every night. The UK will need a 49% increase in electric capacity to cope with this at an approximate cost of £100 billion, possibly collapsing an already antiquated transmission network. It's a similar story with the US but at the expense of $1.4 trillion. Combining this with the plethora of other rising technologies such as super servers, quantum computers, increasing technology levels in India, China and Africa and it is hard to see renewables and gas keeping pace. No other current feasible energy source would be able to sustainably meet these demands other than nuclear. The switch from gas to nuclear will not be quick or easy, however, with the large upfront cost and public opinion making it a very tough sell for governments. To meet the goals of the Paris accord, gas plants will have to have some form of carbon capture and storage (CCS) to prevent CO_2 emissions at the source. This is expensive and when applied to gas plants, the total lifecycle cost between gas CCS and nuclear narrows significant and will only continue to narrow as the relatively infantile nuclear technology develops, meaning nuclear will be economically competitive as a viable option.

To conclude this hugely controversial topic and answer our original hypothesis of what energy production might look like in the future, I will start off with the bold statement that a 100% renewable grid will not be realised because the investments both economically and environmentally outweigh the benefits, especially when potential long-term energy demand growth is considered. Instead, renewables will be used to supplement and reduce usage of current fossil fuel based sources (including nuclear) with new build gas plants replacing coal plants. The type of renewable source employed will depend on geography, with sunny and windy areas utilising solar and wind power respectively. PV will see a continuing increase in numbers with continual price decreases, although this is still largely vulnerable to local subsidies and legislation. At some point, there will have to be some form of carbon tax in order to limit, and hopefully reverse, the inevitable damage rising CO_2 levels will cause, resulting in a disruptive energy movement away from fossil fuels towards renewables and nuclear. There will be a continual battle between renewables, fossil fuels and nuclear power as a result of the three competitive variables, cleanliness, cost, and dependency, nuclear being clean, expensive and dependable, renewables clean, cheap and intermittent and finally fossil fuels dirty, cheap and dependable. Ideally, renewables will be mixed with nuclear; with renewables providing cheap and clean power whilst nuclear provides clean and dependable backup power whilst also ensuring enough energy to meet future demands.

Nuclear

Know What's Watt

Since the world's first nuclear power station was connected to the grid in 1954 in Obninsk, Russia, nuclear power generation has been the subject of much controversy and perhaps misunderstanding. There is no doubting the vast amounts of energy that can be harnessed from nuclear (1 gigawatt of energy production from a coal-fired power station requires 9000 tonnes of coal compared to just 3 kilograms of uranium for a nuclear plant) but there is much concern regarding the safety of nuclear, both short and long-term. This has led to regulatory uncertainty and much opposition both politically and publicly and has stifled the development of new plants, particularly in Western countries. This is a shame. The potential benefit of nuclear power to the whole world holds huge promise and is currently the only practical way of fulfilling human energy needs into the foreseeable future whilst simultaneously eliminating our unsustainable dependency on fossil fuels. Even if nuclear is proven not to be the final answer to sustainable energy, it appears at this point in time to be the most feasible power source to keep the world going until a better source is developed.

There are currently two main types of nuclear reaction from which we can harness energy; fission and fusion. The physics behind these reactions are well documented elsewhere and beyond the scope of this book, but very basically fission splits an atom into two or more lighter ones whilst fusion joins two or more lighter atoms into one heavier atom. During these reactions, energy is released in the form of heat which boils water, creates steam, turns turbines and ultimately produces electricity. The sort of nuclear reactors currently in use utilises fission reactions while fusion reactors remain highly experimental and not yet energy efficient.

The lure behind going nuclear is the huge energy production capability with far fewer environmental consequences than incumbent fossil fuels. Fission electric power stations are actually one of the lowest greenhouse emitting electricity generation methods per unit of energy generated when considering the whole life cycle. A report from the Intergovernmental Panel on Climate Change calculated that nuclear energy produces a staggering 68 times less CO_2 than coal and, rather surprisingly, four times less than solar (mostly due to the chemicals and energy intensive processes required to make solar panels). These incredible statistics certainly haven't gone unnoticed by sharp governments looking to greatly increase their energy producing capabilities. There are currently 440 commercial nuclear reactors currently in use in 31 countries with a further 60 under construction. Combined, they contribute 11% of the world's electricity, already saving the planet from a boatload of CO_2 emissions. The quantity of power generated is set to double by 2040 and the 160 reactors firmly planned certainly support this.

Two-thirds of the generators currently under construction are located in China, India, and Russia, all countries which have an urgent need to fulfil their rapidly expanding populations. China itself has built 30 new reactors since 2002, with 20 new reactors currently under construction, anticipating nuclear to be the most sustainable method to meet the needs of its 1.4bn population. As China matures to first world status, the increase in GDP per capita will ultimately bring about an increase in energy demand already seen in mature economies such as the US and Western Europe. China's nuclear program is becoming so advanced it is now commencing export of its own reactor designs developed as a result of its world-leading reactor R&D.

China will most likely become the dominant force in the design and export of nuclear plants. For now, however, that title goes to Russia and, more specifically, its largest state-owned nuclear power company, Rosatom. Focusing on countries which have no major allegiance to the US or Russia, Rosatom has 33 new plants on its order books, amounting to an investment of $130bn. April 2018 saw Turkey start construction on its first nuclear plant worth some $20bn. Rosatom also has investments in India, Bangladesh, and Hungary. The concern for Western countries is the leverage Russia could wield over these countries when it has so much influence on major energy supplies. The Rooppur facility in Bangladesh, for example, will see Rosatom build a colossal 2400MW plant which would account for over 15% of Bangladesh's total generation capacity. That creates an opportunity for dangerous political leverage should Russia try to use it.

History suggests that it might. In 2015, Russia launched a cyber attack on Ukraine's electrical transmission system causing a power outage for 230,000 people. Fears abound of Russia designing "back doors", such as that used in Ukraine, into its new designs too. Whilst China is on pace to match Russia's dominance, it is also a country where business and politics are closely entwined. In a world where decarbonisation and implementation of cleaner sources of fuel will become increasingly vital, turning to such dominant sources of reactor designs, whose builders have leverage on its political agenda, is a worrying thought. Other countries need to enter the nuclear race if this nuclear political dominance is to be avoided.

India is also ramping up its nuclear capacity but has an even greater urgency to go nuclear than most other countries. A staggering one-third of the population is not connected to any grid network and nearly 20% have no access to electricity at all (2013). Combine these worrying figures with the expected doubling of per capita electricity consumption by 2020, and the huge population growth which will see India become the most populous country by 2024, it is clear India has a monumental challenge ahead of it. With set priorities of economic growth and alleviating poverty, India has seemed to recognise the role nuclear will take in achieving these goals. In May 2017 ten PHWRs (pressurized heavy water reactors) were approved with the aim of achieving 25% nuclear contribution to total electricity by 2050. India has a focused 3 stage program for achieving this.

Stage 1 will see the building of a limited number of PHWRs (Pressurised Heavy Water Reactors) and are important for India as they can utilise natural (unenriched) uranium, eliminating the need to build very expensive uranium enrichment facilities. Plutonium 239 is also an important by-product from these reactions and plays a role in stage 2. A limited number of PHWRs will be built to ensure all reactors have a lifetime's supply of uranium found indigenously to India.

Stage 2 sees the introduction of a new type of reactor; Fast Breeder Reactors (FBRs). Once again FBRs use natural uranium in combination with plutonium 239 created from the PHWRs of stage 1. The plutonium 239 undergoes fission and the neutrons released during this reaction enriches the natural uranium. The magic here is that through enriching natural uranium as part of the reaction, FBRs actually create more fissile (i.e. useable) material than they consume. After multiple cycles in FBRs, the original uranium in stage 1 can produce between 65-128 times more energy than the first reaction.

The final stage utilises thorium based reactors (thermal breeder reactors). Thorium is a weakly radioactive metallic chemical element and is seen as the wonder child of the nuclear world due to the potential benefits it possesses over uranium. I say potential because, despite all the hype, there are currently no large-scale commercial plants up and running on pure thorium. Theoretically, the little amount of Thorium you would need to power the country would solve India's energy needs due to its high abundance in its indigenous Monazite sands. Full utilisation of these reserves is not expected to occur until 2050, however, and even that might be ambitious.

Thorium

Thawing a Nuclear Cold Spell

There are many misconceptions about the wonder that is Thorium. Merely searching the term on the internet provides a plethora of videos and web pages by high flying college professors arguing that thorium is the only sustainable answer to the world's energy needs. Despite the convincing physics, there are reasons why the technology is yet to be utilised. Thorium does, however, offer the potential to pull nuclear out of its current unpopular image as being unsafe and expensive and turn it into a viable source of sustainable potential energy.

Thorium is a radioactive chemical element in much the same way as plutonium and uranium are. It is three to four times more abundant in the Earth's crust than uranium and is found in relatively large quantities in Monazite sands. Monazite sands are where rare earth metals are found, and thorium is currently a by-product from mining these sands. Thorium currently has very little use. India has a predicted 25% of the world's known thorium reserves, but only 2% of global uranium reserves, hence the main reason for India's push for stage 3 Thorium reactors.

Natural thorium is non-fissile (doesn't create a fission reaction) and can only react once it has been enriched with neutrons (remember the stage 2 reaction described earlier). This means it is more stable than other elements and inherently safer in terms of meltdowns. Current uranium reactors create nuclear waste in the form of plutonium 239, which is highly radioactive and has a half-life of 24,000 years (i.e. it takes 24,000 years for just half of the molecules to decay to safe levels). Thorium reactors can utilise plutonium 239 to enrich itself, not only getting rid of the waste reserves of these previously harmful elements but also creating further energy from them. The reactors which utilise thorium are generally more efficient in creating energy. In fact, it is estimated that there is more energy in current thorium reserves then there is in coal, oil and uranium reserves combined.

This all sounds great, but there must be limiting reasons why thorium is not currently in mass use. There are many differing opinions on this, some more plausible than others. Some say development is being suppressed by petrochemical companies who would see a huge decrease in demand for oil. With the colossal amount of money that oil giants spend on lobbying, it is not beyond the realms of possibility. Another interesting thought is that governments want to continue using uranium reactors for their plutonium and uranium waste output, which can be used to make nuclear weapons. Although this may have been the case in the 40's when uranium reactors were first developed, thorium reactors can actually still produce weapons-grade material too. Looking practically there seems to be a much simpler and less conspiracy based explanation; it is simply not economically feasible to produce thorium reactors just yet. It is very similar to the current situation with electric cars; despite being technically very impressive with minimal fuel cost, little maintenance, and no operational pollution; they are still not hugely widespread because they are less practical than incumbent petrol and diesel vehicles. It would be difficult to find a business or government willing to invest such huge upfront sums over multiple decades in an area of rapid technological development such as nuclear when solar and storage prices are continually plummeting. Even uranium is relatively cheap and abundant with many years of foreseeable use. India has a vested interest in developing thorium because of its huge supplies, but for everyone else, it will be better to wait until others develop the technology, and the high costs associated with research and development are spent by others. Unfortunately for nuclear, by the time the technology is developed (2050 best case) it will most likely have already been surpassed by more efficient technologies such as renewables or even other nuclear developments such as the illusive nuclear fusion.

Nuclear Fusion

Light the Fuse

There have been many breakthroughs throughout the past 200 years that have accelerated mankind's progression seemingly overnight. Such electrical inventions as Thomas Edison's light bulb swiftly prompted demand for access to instant electricity, and hence the electrical grid was born. Johannes Gutenberg's printing press enabled hundreds of millions of books to be printed and sparked what we now term "the age of enlightenment". And, of course, the invention of the transistor by Bell Laboratories allowed for the invention of the computer and all its associated developments. Nuclear fusion, when achieved, would certainly have its place amongst these eureka innovations. With a practically infinite supply of clean and safe power, we can once and for all eliminate the scourge of dirty fuels and preserve our planet without compromise. If this all sounds too good to be true, well, it is, for the foreseeable future anyway. Although fusion reactors have been successfully developed and tested, the current design uses more input energy in creating a fusion reaction than is outputted. There are some groups who believe this "ignition" point is just around the corner, while others joke that fusion has been 10 years away for the past 50 years. Whatever the case, the potential and science behind it is certainly encouraging and tangible, with large investments currently exploring the viability of the technology.

As mentioned earlier, fusion reactions release energy in the form of heat by fusing two atoms into one. This is nothing new; fusion has been occurring naturally in the universe for 4.5bn years in the Sun (which is now approximately half way through its lifecycle) and has provided the energy for life on our planet from the first forms of organisms. Fusion occurs in the Sun's core when two protons (lone hydrogen nuclei) fuse together to form helium, releasing some mass in the process which converts to energy. The reason for having such a difficult time commercialising fusion reactions is due to the colossal amount of energy needed to overcome the repelling force of the protons (same charges repel each other) and force them to fuse. The Sun has a slight advantage over us; being 99.8% of the total solar system's mass means there is a huge gravitational force in the core creating temperatures of 15 million degrees centigrade. At this temperature, there is enough energy for some protons to fuse. Replicating this on earth, however, without this huge amount of mass to work with is proving very challenging.

There are currently two leading reactor designs used to create fusion reactions; inertial and magnetic confinement reactors. Inertial confinement fusion (ICF) reactors are real space age stuff, firing very powerful lasers directly into a pellet of fuel with the aim of putting a high enough amount of energy into such a small area that there is enough energy for protons to fuse. The pellet of fuel is usually deuterium-tritium (can be distilled from all forms of water) and a mere pea sized source can create as much electricity as a whole barrel of oil. The actual fusion reaction itself lasts just one-millionth of a second but will yield near 100 times the energy that was used to create the reaction. Furthermore, estimates have arisen stating that a pellet would cost between 25-100 US cents, a much needed concession considering the off-putting cost of constructing such a nuclear plant. The National Ignition Facility (NIF) in California is the most advanced ICF reactor currently testing, having carried out many tests over its lifespan. 2015 saw its most successful test, but still only managed to achieve ⅓ of the necessary energy needed for ignition. ICF reactors are still far from any form of commercial operation.

There is a little more hope, however. The second type of reactor, magnetic confinement reactors, are the most well developed and well funded approaches to fusion and are commonly implemented via a tokamak design. A tokamak is just a fancy (Russian) word for using strong magnetic fields to confine a plasma into the shape of a torus (think hollow donut). These magnetic fields are necessary to keep the plasma (at 300 million degrees Celsius) from touching the walls of the reactor, as touching anything at that temperature would cause instant disintegration. The Joint European Torus (JET) reactor in Oxfordshire, UK, is the largest magnetic confinement reactor and currently holds the record for most energy released from a fusion reaction at 16MW. This resulted from 24MW of total input energy back in 1997, achieving 66% of the ignition target. Although successful in producing energy from fusion, the reactor simply wasn't big enough to create more power than it uses.

This is where we introduce the extravagantly named International Thermonuclear Experimental Reactor. Thankfully we can call it ITER for short. ITER is currently under construction in France and is a similar design to JET; just much bigger and more advanced (the torus chamber will be bigger by a factor of 10). Construction started in 2013 and is planned to be complete in 2021 with plasma experiments starting in 2025 and full deuterium-tritium experiments in 2035. ITER is a very significant project for many reasons. Firstly, it aims to generate 500MW of output energy from 50MW of input for 500 seconds (approximately 8 minutes). This results in what's called a Q value of 10 (where Q=1 is break-even point), meaning we can generate ten times the energy we put in. It also represents the combination of all knowledge and experiments on fusion so far, drawing from all the results of previous experiments (such as JET), representing our very best attempt to reach this breakeven point. It does seem, however, to be a last attempt at proving the commercial viability of nuclear fusion, as the eye-watering $16 billion it is estimated to have cost, is a huge risk for the sponsoring bodies (EU, India, Japan, China, Russia, South Korea, and the US) who see controversial topics such as nuclear energy high risk. As the technology and concept behind fusion are still relatively primitive, there are still a lot of unknown unknowns, i.e. we don't know a lot of what we don't know. These problems are inevitable and will only arise after experimentation has started. Whether these problems are serious enough to completely disprove the concept is obviously unknown, but they could certainly be serious enough to make it commercially unviable. Even if all goes well and the break-even point is achieved, it will still take around 10 years worth of research and development and materials testing to transform it into a usable form. However, we cannot sit idle and wait for the answer to fall into our laps; we must go and seek these answers. If it is proven viable, it would be the scientific breakthrough of the century, bringing enough energy to pull whole countries out of darkness and into a new super productive era.

Chapter Summary

Concerning energy, one thing is certain. Without change to our current trajectory, our reliance on fossil fuels will cause irreparable damage to our environment and a significant reduction in quality of life. Finite fossil fuels such as coal, oil, and gas are insufficient to meet future energy demands. Innovations such as electric vehicles will be mandated to reduce damaging greenhouse gases but at the expense of increased electrical demand from an already stretched and large fossil fuel dependant distribution system. Meeting demand from developing countries such as China and India will prove to be very challenging and fossil fuels, especially coal, will likely be seen by short-sighted and cash-strapped governments as the only feasible option to overcome this hurdle.

Renewables can be very advantageous in supplementing current dispatchable power sources; solar and wind offer particularly efficient solutions when hybridised and applied to local climates which allow for high utilisation rates. The use of too many renewable sources, however, proves both too costly and inefficient. The higher the proportion of power generated from renewables the larger the overcapacity factor needs to be; 100% reliance on renewable sources would need to be scaled to 10 times that of peak demand to overcome the issue of intermittency. At this level of investment, both the costs and life-cycle CO_2 production would be far too high to be anywhere near practical. Instead, a compromise between the convenience of the already commissioned dispatchable plants, such as natural gas, should be hybridised with renewable sources where the geography proves optimal. This will quickly and cost-effectively allow for a near immediate drop in CO_2 levels and when combined with CCS systems, will hopefully prove sufficient to meet the Paris Climate Accord target of ensuring temperature rises remain below the 2-degree target.

Looking further into the future for a more sustainable long-term approach, nuclear energy presents the most promising compromise between cost, production capability, and pollution. Although the current initial costs of creating nuclear power plants tend to make it prohibitively expensive, future improvements in the technology, a desperate need to reduce environmental damage, and the meeting of high future energy demands, may force nuclear plants into mass use. The combination of nuclear and renewables will perhaps offer the best compromise, as over-reliance on a single fuel source is never ideal. Unfortunately, major change, such as that needed in the energy sector, is rarely proactive; instead, it tends to be reactive upon disasters. It, therefore, may be the case that things get a lot worse before they get better, with severe weather episodes and major blackouts the drivers for change. There is hope on the horizon, however, current technology allows for a safe course of action for those who are brave enough to invest heavily upfront. In an era of austerity and low funding in science and technology, this change may come later than it should. Hopefully, it won't be too little too late.

6. Genomics and Gene Modification

Engineering the Future

So far we have seen a variety of technologies, inventions, and innovations that are poised to significantly change our daily lives in a (hopefully) beneficial way. From autonomous vehicles to power plants, they have all focused on external objects and their influence on our lives. But what about change and innovation from within? Can we engineer and modify our genetic blueprint to develop a superior version of ourselves? How far can we go and how will it affect society? Genomics is in such an infant stage that these questions are still only just starting to be asked let alone solved, but it is a fascinating avenue to pursue. The most fundamental essence of life is evolution and the survival of the fittest so it is only natural that man attempts to speed up this dawdling evolutionary process and engineer their own future. Genomics marks a new chapter in the history of humankind where genetic human traits are no longer simply passed down from parents via natural processes but are selected, engineered and maximised through choice and science. Is a world full of genetically perfect humans even desirable? Isn't variety the spice of life? Sometimes there is only one way to find out.

The Basics

DNA, genes, genomes? What's the difference?

Before venturing into the fantastical future of genetic modification it is important to first understand the basics of the science behind it and how this knowledge can be exploited to do what was hitherto impossible; modify our genetic blueprint.

Let's start from the most basic of components; amino acids. Amino acids are simple organic compounds containing both a carboxyl (—COOH) and an amino (—NH$_2$) group. They are the basic building blocks of all life which connect in a multitude of combinations to create an array of proteins with differing but very specific purposes. These proteins (along with other chemicals) combine to create different cells, these cells combine to make tissues, tissues make organs and organs create living creatures. The structure of a protein, however, needs to be very specifically arranged in order to fulfil its intended and necessary function, such as the antibody protein which binds to specific foreign particles, such as bacteria and viruses, to help the body fight off infections. This is where DNA comes in. DNA (or the rather long-winded deoxyribonucleic acid) cleverly tells the amino acids how to arrange themselves in order to create the necessary proteins. The only problem here is that a cell is split into two main components; a nucleus where the DNA is held and a surrounding cytoplasm housing the amino acids. The DNA strands are too large to fit between the cytoplasm (where the amino acids are held) and the nucleus (where all DNA is held). For a cell to continue to grow and multiply, there needs to be a way for the DNA to reach the amino acids in order for further proteins to be made. This is where nature gets clever. Special chemicals in the nucleus create smaller copies of particular segments of DNA called RNA (ribonucleic acid). These RNA molecules are small enough to fit through the pores of the nucleus into the cytoplasm where another chemical, ribosomes, await. Ribosomes are protein building machines and read the RNA strands 3 letters at a time to enable it to suck in amino acids, combine them into the correct combination and length to create proteins, which in turn go on to fulfil their function in the development of the living organism. These letters referred to are the nucleotides which form the fundamental component of DNA. They come in four "flavours"; adenine (A), guanine (G), cytosine (C) and thymine (T). These four sugar chemicals attach to each other to form a base pair, all held together by a sugar-phosphate backbone to form a long strand of bases. Two lengths of this strand intertwine in a very space efficient manner to create what we commonly refer to as the double helix. These long strands wrap to create chromosomes, of which every cell has 46; 23 from mum and 23 from dad. Interestingly, all DNA in a single cell, if unwound, would stretch 2 meters and all DNA from all cells in a body would stretch about the diameter of the entire solar system, twice. This is equal to travelling to the sun and back four times or to the moon and back 1500 times. These somewhat silly comparisons show the sheer magnitude of information necessary to build a human being.

There is a lot of complex chemistry to grasp there, but fundamentally DNA (and hence the smaller bite-size RNA strands) consists of nucleotides (A, C, T, G) which ribosomes read to convert amino acids into proteins which form the fundamental building blocks of life. The arrangement of the nucleotide bases is what decides which protein to form. From this understanding can genes now be defined. A gene is simply the arrangement of these bases which combine to make a single functional unit of DNA. Genes such as blue eyes, brown hair and even taste in food all result from different but specific combinations of bases to create every individual. The collection of all your genes creates the genome which represents all the genetic information of an organism. To help clarify the difference, imagine genes as sentences in a book. The sentences may make sense of their own but there is no context; you need to read every sentence in a book in the correct order to understand the story. The genome would thus be the whole book and only by reading all sentences in the book does the context make sense. Whereas with genes we look at exactly what function they are responsible for (blue eyes for example), with genomes we have to look at how these genes interact with other and the holistic effect they have on the organism they serve to form.

Genomics

Playing God?

Based on everything we now know, genomics can be best described as the study of genes and how they function. An all-encompassing field, it deals directly with the science of structure, function, evolution, mapping and, perhaps most importantly, editing of genomes. It is a relatively modern field and has only recently shown great potential after the first successful complete sequencing of a human genome in April 2003 after nearly a decade of work. Starting in 1995, the map of a human's 20,500 genes took hundreds of scientists across dozens of countries many years and over $3bn to complete. This map was a goldmine for medical researchers who now had access to a set of instructions for a healthy and fully functioning human. The sources and causes of diseases could be identified at a genetic level and work is now underway by researchers across the globe to find ways to identify and treat illnesses and diseases at this most fundamental genetic level.

One of the most beneficial results of this discovery is the ability to predict, diagnose and treat conditions at an individual level, creating very specific prognoses based on an individual's genetic circumstances. Instead of treating illness with the typical one size fits all approach, precise treatments can be offered based on the individual's genetic situation. This should mean fewer drugs and treatments as well as more effective and less intrusive solutions.

Time has once again worked its magic on the cost of technology. From its impractical high of $3bn for the sequencing of a single genome, costs today have dropped to nearer the $1000 mark. It is widely regarded that with a little more influence from competition and technological innovation this cost will further drop to under $100, a point where most people will be able to afford to have their full and personal genome analysed.

Progress is being made in leaps and bounds in the field. The Broad Institute in Cambridge, Massachusetts, claims that during the month of October 2016 it decoded the equivalent of one human genome every 32 minutes, resulting in a collection of over 200 terabytes of raw genetic data. Although this is much smaller than the scale of information handled by internet companies, it creates complex storage problems for biologists and hospitals. Cloud storage companies have already spotted this potential market and offer to store your whole genome (a file between 100-400GB) for a mere $25 a year, equating to just 2 cents per GB per month. The national cancer institute had already announced it will move its 2.6 petabyte Cancer Genome Atlas into the cloud at a cost of $19 million. By placing this data on the cloud medical researchers could be allowed access to the anonymised data in the hope of comparing and analysing the masses of data to help further understand the effect of different genes, hopefully resulting in better treatments for everyone. Many countries such as the UK, US, France, and even Estonia have funded programmes to help bring the benefits into the realm of reality.

Despite being in the early stages of infancy, gene therapy is already being trialled with varying success. Take haemophilia, a mostly inherited genetic disorder that impairs the body's ability to make blood clots and therefore stop bleeding. A small trial used an adeno-associated viral vector (tools commonly used by molecular biologists to deliver genetic material into cells) to deliver a gene for Factor IX (the missing clotting protein) to liver cells. Somewhat a success, most of the patients now made at least some Factor IX and had fewer bleeding accidents. Severe Combined Immune Deficiency (SCID), more colloquially known as bubble boy disease after the heartbreaking story of David Vetter in 1971, is also now being tackled genetically. David was born in Houston, Texas with SCID, a deadly disease which meant David was born without an effective immune system. Any bacteria or virus entering his system could quickly prove fatal. Mere seconds after birth he was forced into the confines of a sterilised bubble where bacteria and viruses, which lurk in the natural atmosphere, couldn't enter his system. The only known solution at the time was a bone marrow transplant from a close matched donor, of which was hoped by his sister but was later found to be unsuitable. With no available options, 12 years passed David and his family by being confined to a bubble and devoid of direct contact with anyone and anything outside his bubble. Science had progressed enough by 1984; however, to attempt a bone marrow transplant from a less identical match and the surgery itself was a success. In a cruel twist of fate, David died 15 days later from a cancer lying undetected in his sister's bone marrow. It was the first time scientists discovered cancer was caused by a virus. Gene therapy allowed a recent trial in Italy to introduce a gene called ADA into the bone marrow cells of patients affected by the disease in the laboratory. These genetically corrected cells were then transplanted back into the cells of the patients to identify the effect on their immune systems. Then immune systems were reconstituted in all six of the patients without noticeable side effects and all patients are now living normal healthy lives without the need for further care.

Gene therapy could also be set to aid the uphill struggle against one of the most revered diseases of all, cancer. 38.4% of all people are estimated to be diagnosed with some form of cancer in their lifetime, often resulting in a horrific, lonely and undignified end to life, not just for the patient but also their family, of which I can personally attest to. Two-thirds of all gene therapy trials are for cancer and while most are in the early exploratory stages, many are now entering the advanced stages of trialling through multiple techniques. There are three main directions which scientists are focusing their efforts.

The first technique uses genetically engineered viruses which are modified to kill the cancer cells directly without affecting any other healthy cells. Studies on animals have proved fairly successful for targeting a variety of cancers such as colon, bladder and bone cancer. Although successful in animals, the viruses used in the study were found to be fought off by the human immune system and would, therefore, be killed before they had a chance to target the cancer cells. The tests at least offer a proof of concept, however. With further time and experience, the opportunities could be profound.

A second method is gene transfer where a foreign gene is introduced into targeted cancer cells with the aim of killing them directly or by preventing the cancer cells from funnelling blood to the surrounding tumours, thereby killing them. In animal studies, gene transfer techniques proved successful for treating prostate, lung and pancreatic cancer.

A third promising approach is immunotherapy which seeks to enhance the body's own ability to fight cancer. In clinical trials, immunotherapy has already proved successful in fighting leukaemia and lymphoma in children but with some severe side effects. Cancer vaccines are also being explored where tumour cells from an infected patient are extracted, engineered with genes that cause them to be more susceptible to the immune system and then reinserted into the patient where the newly modified cells better fight the tumour cells. All methods are merely scratching the surface of what is possible, however, and it is almost certain that future results will prove very effective in the fight against cancer.

CRISPR

Cut, Copy and Paste

Of course, all of the above trials and techniques are only possible once the necessary technology becomes viable. Confidence in gene therapy as a viable cure has recently been renewed largely in part to a new gene-modifying technique called CRISPR (Clustered Regularly Interspaced Short Palindromic Repeats). CRISPR is a system that can be programmed to locate and target specific stretches of genetic code, cut them out and replace them with working code to rid the body of the DNA that was malfunctioning and causing the illness or disease. Although the capacity to edit genes has been around for decades, CRISPR has transformed the field by reducing the costs of engineering by 99% and reducing the time taken from years to weeks. The highly programmable nature of CRISPR makes the system beautifully simple and flexible. Researchers can now edit genes in living cells, opening up a future possibility for editing human genomes at precise locations in a living patient.

Despite being simple to program and use, the biology behind CRISPR is quite complex but truly fascinating. When people refer to CRISPR they're probably referring to CRISPR-Cas9, a complex of enzymes which have been acting as a defence system against viral infections in nature for millions of years. Bacteria have evolved to fight viruses and stop them from taking their natural path of replicating until the targeted cell is overwhelmed. Bacteria counter the viral invasion by deploying waves of DNA-cutting proteins to cut the viral genes. Any bacteria which survives the viral onslaught will then incorporate the loose snippets of viral DNA into its own genome so it can spot the virus quicker if it were ever to return. By knowing the genetic coding of the invader, the bacteria can now fight the virus more effectively by sending out the cas9 enzyme working in tandem with a copy of the viral RNA and snip the offending code to stop the virus from replicating and spreading.

All this occurs naturally and forms the basis of our immune system, but researches are now looking for ways to program the CRISPR-Cas9 enzymes to find specific lines of code suspected to cause a disease or illness. Researchers can design their own RNA code to attach to any series of genetic code, such as a line of code suspected to be causing harm. This designed RNA code can then be mixed with the Cas9 enzyme and inserted into a living cell to either take the offending gene out of commission or repair the defective gene to allow it to properly perform its intended function. The system is not yet perfect and there have been mixed results. The enzyme has been found to occasionally make cuts in the wrong place, thereby disturbing healthy genes, but the system certainly offers a feasible method to explore editing genes in living cells.

Multiple companies are already utilising CRSIPR to diagnose genomes. Health company Human Longevity Inc. now offers an eight-hour physical exam called the Health Nucleus. Costing $25,000, it consists of an inside-and-out examination that includes whole-genome sequencing, high tech scanning, and early diagnostics. So far the company has sequenced 40,000 genomes with demand rising and claims that one in 40 will discover they have an unknown serious cancer. As the cost and duration of these tests decrease, expect these sorts of examinations to become more common.

While simple sequencing using CRISPR is becoming more prominent, editing and modifying genomes using the technique has proved much more challenging. There have been three attempts in China to edit the genome in live cells. The first two in 2015 and 2016 were conducted on non-viable embryos (they could never have resulted in a live birth) whilst the third was conducted on a viable embryo that theoretically could have resulted in a live birth. Despite CRISPR being known for its precision, the trials resulted in off-target mutations where wrong parts of the genome were cut. The first Chinese team successfully edited a diseased gene in only 5% of embryos with the second team performing even worse. This goes to show that despite our grasping of the theory and science, the real world introduces difficulties only time and experience can solve and shows that, despite the hype, the technology is still very much in its infancy.

Researchers have targeted their efforts on the HIV gene too, showing much potential. In 2015 scientists managed to cut the HIV gene from laboratory samples, proving the concept. The following year saw the trial extended to live mice that were infected with the HIV virus in 99% of their cells. Injecting a CRISPR enzyme compound into the tails removed more than 50% of the infected cells from the test samples. Despite the success, there is still a steep hill to climb but it is certainly worth exploring the viable premise that CRISPR or similar techniques could one day rid the world of HIV and other nasty genetic diseases.

Eugenics

Next gene-eration

There is a fundamental problem with all we've discussed so far on the topic. Eliminating cancer or HIV in a patient is clearly important and worthwhile, but since those modified genes die with the patient, so too do the benefits. The modification of defective genes will be an ongoing battle for as long as humans are born according to nature, with genetic defects. Instead of editing genes after birth where suffering has a chance to take hold, would it ultimately be more advantageous to modify genomes before birth? This very question is the basis of the field of eugenics; a movement that is concerned with improving the genetic composition of the human race. We have been living with selective breeding in dogs and agriculture for decades now, enjoying the benefits of canine friends with the most desirable traits such as intelligence, strength, and longevity bred into them. Yet when we consider doing the same to humans, a large moral and ethical dilemma looms over us. Whilst the extremes are clearly defined (eliminating cancer is an obligation but the creation of a master race is to be avoided at all costs) where do we draw these genetic red lines and when is too much too much?

While gene therapy changes the genome of somatic cells (cells which aren't reproductive cells), these cells are not within the germline and therefore the traits are non-heritable. Human germline modification, therefore, focuses on the editing of the genome in such a way that it is heritable and can be passed down to following generations, in other words creating genetically modified people. Whilst we have successfully genetically modified plants and animals, modifying human genomes has mostly been strictly off-limits for safety and ethical reasons, with over 40 countries prohibiting it unconditionally. One of the main issues is the high-risk unknown outcomes of any attempts; we have already seen how Chinese trials on living cells created unexplained off-target mutations. Any error, whether known or unknown, will be passed on through reproduction and unintended mutations and defects may be introduced. Any future application of this technology must therefore be strictly aligned with adequate scientific and social controls before germline modification can safely be integrated into society. The ability to modify genomes prior to birth opens the floodgates to the controversy of designer babies and the picking and choosing of their genes and traits. Although this, at present, is certainly a long way off, it will become an important issue as soon as the technology is possible and it is imperative that legislation and regulation are introduced to protect the rights of, not only the affected child but also the genetic integrity of the human race as a whole.

Designer Babies

Designer genes - Fashion or Fascism?

The ability to pick and choose the genetic traits of children splits opinion to the extremes. Whether ultimately beneficial or detrimental to the future of mankind it is thought-provoking at the very least. Although the issues surrounding designer babies have been debated for decades, new developments from innovations such as CRISPR have reignited the flame of curiosity and researchers, both scientific and philosophical, have delved deeper into the societal repercussions from the introduction of such techniques.

Whilst there is no argument that elimination of degenerative diseases such as multiple sclerosis, Parkinson's disease, and HIV should be progressed as fast as possible, how do we distinguish between therapeutic applications and those which might be considered vain, cosmetic and unnecessary. If being born short, wide and with a funny voice leads one to be bullied, resulting in mental anxiety and a lower quality of life, would this be considered a therapeutic necessity or purely cosmetic? There is also the problem of social inequality; those who can afford to edit genomes will most likely benefit more than those who cannot. If a child has traits of strength and intelligence bred into them, it is surely logical for an employer to favour those who will perform better on paper? This would breed a cycle of enrichment for those who are wealthy enough to afford germline modification in the first place, ultimately leading to a new class of civilisation such as that explored in the film Gattaca.

Perhaps the most sensitive ethical issue found in a future of a genetically altered race is the termination of embryos deemed of too low of a quality for reproduction but may very well, given a chance, have grown to fulfil a rich and eventful life as is every human's right. As unfair as picking and choosing of life may sound, society is, in fact, doing exactly this right now, just much more subtly. Every year 4.1 million babies are born in the US. Statistically, 1 in 700 of these will be born with Down syndrome where an extra copy of chromosome 21 is present. A journal from EMBO Reports 2006 titled "the future of neo-eugenics" presents the argument that we are already terminating embryos deemed defective at a surprisingly high rate. The paper states that although 6150 babies are expected to be born with Down syndrome, in reality only 4370 are; the others were aborted during pregnancy. This represents a 29% abortion rate in Atlanta, GA, and Hawaii where statistics on this subject are available. Across the globe, 75% of Down syndrome foetuses were aborted in Southern Australia, 80% in Taiwan and 85% in Paris, France. It is not just Down syndrome where there is a high rate of abortion either; data from the European Surveillance of Congenital Abnormalities shows that between 1995 and 1999 about 40% of infants with any one of 11 main congenital (a disease or physical abnormality present from birth) disorders were aborted in Europe. Whether well-intentioned or not, the elimination of genetically defective foetuses through abortion is eugenic in both intention and effect as the parent has replaced the defective foetus with the hope of a genetically superior baby in a subsequent birth. Why is the screening and genetic selection of all embryos any different? The result is the same; producing the healthiest baby possible.

The genetic screening of embryos is occurring at an increasing rate, although current legislation limits this to purely medical reasoning. PGD (Pre-implantation genetic diagnosis) is a treatment which genetically profiles embryos prior to implementation. The embryos are tested in the lab and, upon being found defect-free from the 400 or so conditions tested for, are placed back in the womb via IVF where the embryo grows into a healthy child. The screening of embryos is currently limited to parents who have ended previous pregnancies due to a serious genetic condition, the family has a history of a serious genetic condition or if the parent already has a child with a serious genetic condition and wants to avoid the same condition upon having a further child. It is conceivable that one day every person has, as an embryo, survived a PGD screening with many unborn embryos failing the make the cut. There are only two tangible barriers to mass screening via PGD; legislation and cost. As noted previously, screens are currently limited to those who would medically benefit from it. PGD and the succeeding IVF procedure is expensive; a course of IVF in the UK costs between £7,000 to £10,000 which, although a lot of money, is cheaper than caring for a special needs child (from birth until the age of 18) which is estimated to be four times as expensive ($1m) than caring for genetically healthy child ($240,000). This cost saving would not only be economical for individual parents but also to universal health care systems such as Britain's NHS, which is already in desperate need of cost-cutting techniques. There is also the point that nature has developed a much cheaper and more enjoyable way to procreate.

Many countries currently completely prohibit PGD screening in any form including Germany, Austria, Ireland, and Switzerland whilst most others limit it to strictly medical purposes such as Belgium, France, Greece, and the UK. As with most controversial innovations, however, as the benefits of the new technology become clearer and the doomsday scenarios preached by antagonists fail to materialise, the practice will gradually become more and more accepted and adopted into normal societal behaviours. Germline modification will spread rapidly once the first wave of designer babies appears as parents seek to compete with others for the most superior child.

A Genetic Future

A Leopard Can't Change its Spots... or Can it?

Letting our minds wander, what might a future in which humans are bred for success look like? Many might reasonably assume that key traits such as intelligence, strength, height, and confidence would be the first checkboxes ticked on the genetic shopping list. In practice, these traits are extremely difficult to isolate and alter because none of these talents arise from a single gene mutation. Scientists estimate that height is influenced by as many as 93,000 genetic variations with only 697 of them currently identified. Genes are also thoroughly interconnected, potentially making the editing of some genes incredibly difficult without affecting the properties of others. It may, in theory, be possible to alter these complex and interconnected traits but the science to do so is certainly a fair few years off, and medical legislature many more years after that.

PGD and IVF also open the door to further controversial practices. "Saviour siblings" are the brothers or sisters of a child which are born with the intention of medically assisting a pre-existing child. By PGD screening fertilized embryos for genetic compatibility against an existing child, a genetically defect free and close matched embryo can be selected and born via IVF. This saviour sibling can "donate" life-saving tissues or even transplant whole organs and cells. In the United Kingdom, The Human Fertilisation and Embryology Authority (HFEA) has already ruled for the lawfulness of creating a saviour sibling using modern reproductive techniques and a number of success stories have already come to light. There are moral considerations to make for the donor child who has to live with the disconcerting knowledge of having been brought into this world with the intention of essentially being spare parts for another child. For most families this might not be the case; if parents were to want a second subsequent child why not exploit science to at least have the option to donate to the other child? As long as the rights of the saviour sibling are considered and they are not forced into donating tissue or organs against their will, or quality of life for their sibling compromised, the practice has the ability to reduce the reliance on organs from random donors, which is already stretched, to become a secure and reliable source of medical aid.

Perhaps the most controversial effects of advanced and widespread germline modification would be a societal gap between genetic "haves" and "have-nots". Although the current legislature limits the use of genetic modification to purely medical reasoning, it isn't too difficult to imagine a time where control of all genetic possibilities is in the hands of the parents. As long as there is a market demand (there are certainly many parents who would opt for genetic modification of their children) there will be a potential supply, limited only by government rules and regulation. If it were ever possible to enhance the muscle mass, strength and intelligence of a human it would put the beneficiaries at the top of the pile for almost any application, whether it be college admissions or job applications. Although both college and job admissions already screen for desirable traits such as intelligence and social skills they are based on results (SAT scores or interview skills), not on genetics. Some college students might be more genetically intelligent than others but, without putting in the necessary study time, they might obtain a lower result than a student with a lower natural intelligence but a better work ethic. This second student who is now able to put a better real-world result on their resume is more likely (and deserving) of obtaining a job than the first genetically gifted but less hard-working student. If this resume were now to prove that student A was genetically more intelligent than student B, despite the poorer result, it could be expected that some employers would prefer the better natural talent. This is the biggest social issue to overcome as those with the means to create genetically superior children will create a superior class of humans who will, in turn, create more genetically superior children, creating an elite class at the expense of those who do not have access to the technology.

Even if all germline modifications were prohibited, the fact that the genome can be sequenced would still cause the same issue. Instead of those who can afford to modify genes prospering, those with a superior natural genome sequence would benefit most at the expense of those with inferior genomes. Whether this is regarded as unfair or just an extension of evolution and survival of the fittest, however, is up for debate.

Whichever path genetic modification ends up taking, it is very clear that thorough rules and regulations need to be clearly created and stringently enforced. Autocratic and totalitarian regimes such as North Korea and China wouldn't think twice about creating a superhuman nation in an effort to assert world dominance of their communist regimes. One can only imagine what horrors the Nazi regime would have concocted had they access to germline modification. Could the telomerase enzymes in lobsters' DNA (which protects the end of their chromosomes) be utilised to reproduce in humans the anti-aging properties for which lobsters are known for? Could future astronauts have their genes tailored for interplanetary travel as we approach an era of space and planetary exploration? Only time will tell.

Possession of superior genes doesn't automatically correlate to a better future; nature is only half the battle; nurture provides the rest. But there is no doubting the benefits that genetic modification will bring to those who are suffering and the potential future hardship it could eliminate as cruel diseases and illnesses are removed at the source. At this present moment, however, your selfish author is primarily concerned with modifying the embarrassing gene linked to male baldness!

7. Bionics

BCI (Brain Computer Interface)

Taking Mind-Body Connection to a Whole New Level

Technological fields such as AI, driverless cars and robotics often measure success in terms of parity to human intelligence and functionality, with AI voice systems such as Apple's Siri and Amazon's Alexa aiming to engage its users in lifelike conversation. But instead of striving to make machine more like man, what about the antithetical approach of making man more machine? This is the essence of bionics; the study of mechanical systems that function like living organisms or parts of living organisms and opens conceptual possibilities once thought to remain thoroughly in the realms of science fiction.

Brain-computer interfaces (BCIs) are conceptually simple; a direct communication pathway between the organic brain and external devices. To date, BCIs have mostly sought to research, map and repair human cognitive functions ranging from robotic arms connected directly to the CNS (central nervous system) for a sense of touch and environmental feedback to neuro-prosthetic applications, including the restoration of damaged hearing, sight, and movement. Although still very much in its infancy, BCI research is increasingly turning to more disruptive functions such as assisting, augmenting and improving brain functionality and capability, in essence creating a cyborg-like superbeing which is more capable than the natural body.

UCLA Professor, Jacque Vidal, is often credited as the most prominent pioneer of BCIs and has numerous peer-reviewed publications on the topic, such as his 1977 success in controlling a cursor-like graphical object on a computer screen using signals emitted from the brain. 23 years later in 2000, Miguel Nicolelis of Duke University, North Carolina and his team successfully developed an innovative BCI that could decode the brain activity in owl monkeys (monkeys make for excellent test subjects due to their advanced hand manipulation and grasping abilities) and translate this activity to movements in a robotic arm. Videos online can be viewed of a monkey using nothing but the power of thought to move a robotic arm away from itself to grasp a treat and the corresponding return journey to its mouth. Since then numerous academics have been able to capture brain motor cortex signals to control external devices.

We have come a long way from monkeys feeding themselves with a third robotic limb, however. In 2005, tetraplegic Matt Nagel became the first person to control a robotic hand through the use of a BCI as part of a pioneering trial of Cybernetics's BrainGate implanted chip. The 96 electrode chip allowed for control of not just an external limb but also a computer cursor, lights, and television just by the power of Nagel's thought alone.

There are three main classifications of BCIs based on the invasiveness of the implant within the brain. Non-invasive BCIs sit outside the scalp and are usually electrode pads or caps fixed directly to the skin using electroencephalogy (EEG) monitoring methods to record electrical activity outside the brain. Non-invasive BCIs have demonstrated the ability to control cursors, robotic arms, drones and even brain to brain communication. All three levels of BCIs trade invasiveness for signal clarity; non-invasive BCIs record the weakest signal clarity due to the signal distorting effects of the skull but are clearly the safest. Despite the weaker signal clarity, EEG recording techniques have proved surprisingly successful, mostly due to its fine temporal resolution, ease of use, low setup cost and portability. The weak signal, however, currently limits the use of EEG to laboratory type conditions where external noise levels, which interfere with the results, can be controlled. The users also have to be trained to perform the tasks at hand with full unbroken concentration.

Partially invasive BCIs are the next tier where the implant is placed inside the skull but outside of the delicate grey matter of the brain. As you might expect, signal strength is greater under the cranium bone but inserting the electrode underneath is significantly less safe as there is a risk of scar tissue forming around the implant as the body rejects the foreign body. Electrocorticography (ECoG) measures the electrical activity of the brain in a similar fashion to EEG but the electrodes are placed inside a small plastic pad that sits above the cortex and below the dura mater (a membrane in the brain). ECoG technologies were first trialled in humans in 2004 where a teenage boy was able to play space invaders using nothing but thought. The trial found that control is rapid, requires minimal training and may prove to be the best compromise between invasiveness and control.

Lastly, we have fully invasive BCIs which sit deep in the grey matter of the brain, resulting in the best signal quality of the three forms of BCI. An early attempt at implanting a fully invasive BCI into a human was in 1978 when a blind man "Jerry" had a 68 electrode sensor placed into his visual cortex. The implant produced phosphenes (phosphenes are the fuzzy patches of colour you see when you rub your eyes too hard or look at the sun) which allowed him to experience the sensation of seeing light. A second generation of this implant was then placed into a different blind man in 2002 where Jens Naumann became the first in a series of 16 paying patients to receive the implant. Whereas the first implant allowed merely for the sensation of light, this updated chip restored Jens' vision (albeit imperfectly) and allowed him to drive a vehicle around a car park at slow speeds.

As progress is made and a better understanding of the brain and its workings is obtained we will see BCI technologies expand beyond the current restorative functions in disabled people to augmentation of perfectly healthy ones. This will allow man to go beyond its natural limits, becoming quicker, more knowledgeable and, hopefully, more productive.

The not too distant future looks promising for non-invasive BCIs, the easiest of all BCIs to experiment on. MIT Media Lab is currently experimenting with a "wearable silent speech system for silent and seamless natural language communication with other devices and people". Named AlterEgo, the tech rests on the wearer's ear, jaw and mouth. The slick looking device uses electrodes to pick up neuromuscular signals which are triggered upon subvocalizing (when you say words in your head). Essentially the system uses artificial intelligence designed to correlate particular signals released from the brain with words or phrases, thus allowing for silent communication with an AI assistant. MIT Media Lab have successfully demonstrated the device with the user navigating TV channels. Although the useful applications of this technology may currently be rather limited, the proof of concept of reading brain signals (although currently indirectly) has been proved. Where the tech takes us from here is limited to the imagination and ingenuity of developers and entrepreneurs.

Looking further into the future, however, and the prospects can quickly start to look illusory or even deluded. The technology has been credited with opening potential applications from silent mind-to-mind communication to the reading of other people's memories. You may dismiss this as barmy, but, as we will see when we delve deeper into the science behind this technology, it does not appear as far-fetched as it may sound.

In late 2016, biomedical engineer and neuroscientist Dr. Theodore Berger and entrepreneur Bryan Johnson joined forces to start the neurotechnology company Kernal. Dr. Berger had previously broken major ground in obtaining results from brain implants when he identified and manipulated the neuron firing sequences in rats. A rat's hippocampus (responsible for the consolidation of information of long and short-term information) fires neuron patterns that generate a code which the brain recognises as a long-term memory. Dr. Berger, therefore, trained rats to perform a specific task and measured the subsequent neuron codes resulting from the rat "remembering" how to complete the task. Unsurprisingly, stronger neural codes were recorded from rats that completed the task quicker and easier than from those which "forgot". The real development from this experiment, however, was when Dr. Berger manually fired the strong codes (learned by AI algorithms) back into the rats' hippocampus in an experiment where the rat had to pull a lever for some food. Remarkably the rats who had previously forgotten how to pull the lever remembered after having the code manually fired into their brains. Dr. Berger essentially inserted a memory into the rat.

Kernal, and the army of other nascent BCI upstarts have seemingly spotted the game-changing disruptive potentials of this technology and are desperately seeking ways to bring BCI technology into commercial reality. Leading the charge alongside Johnson is Mark Zuckerberg, the US military agency Darpa and Elon Musk.

The potential applications of BCI technologies are far-reaching and limited only by the creativity of entrepreneurs and scientists. Mind to mind communication has understandably long been thought to be purely in the realm of fantasy. A recent experiment by a team of neuroscientists in Spain has developed a system that allows a person to transmit the words "hola" and "chao" from a laboratory in India to one in France using nothing but thought. EEG equipment picked up the brain signals from the sender who subvocalized these words and converted the corresponding signals into 0s and 1s. These signals were then sent via the internet to the other side of the world in France. Upon receiving the digital information, a clever device translated the binary coding into a format which could be induced into the recipient's brain. This clever device uses TMS (Transcranial Magnetic Stimulation), a clever non-invasive technique which uses a changing magnetic field to induce an electrical current to a small targeted region of the brain via electromagnetic induction, effectively stimulating brain activity. This stimulation then activates phosphenes, which appears to the user as flashes of light despite there being no direct light involved. A phosphene appearance represents a "1" and no phosphene appearance represents a "0", from which the recipient can translate into words or meaning. Many have played down this experiment by likening it to a fancy way of sending Morse code, which is hard to deny. Looking at the bigger picture, however, information has successfully been transmitted from one mind to another without any direct contact. That is a deeply impressive feat and creates a strong foundation for others to build upon. I can reasonably foresee a future (once the technology becomes small and powerful enough) where wearable devices (or even implants) will be used regularly for mind to mind communication, effectively operating a mobile phone from within your brain.

One of the most immediate barriers to the progress of brain implant technology is one which has plagued the medical industry for centuries; the body's resistance to foreign bodies entering it. When brain implants were tested in pigs, the animal's immune system responded by forming adhesions (scar tissues). The body's natural reaction to foreign bodies, such as splinters, is to either degrade the object if it is organic and easy to break down or inflame the area in order to create new skin cells under the foreign object and push it towards the skin's surface until it is removed. It is obviously not possible to do this in the brain; a metal implant cannot be degraded by the chemicals in the body or pushed out through the cranium. The only other available defence mechanism is to completely surround the body with scar tissue to shield it from the rest of the body. Scar tissue in the limited space of the brain can cause restriction and lead to serious issues. Researchers are therefore teaming up with biomaterial specialists and surgeons to develop new coatings and techniques to improve the body's tolerance to implants.

Neuralink, another of serial entrepreneur Elon Musk's ambitious start-ups, aims to bypass this problem through the use of a dystopian sounding "neural lace". Neuralink is a medical research company committed to merging the human brain with intelligent computers. The neural lace consists of very thin (on the nanometer scale) electric meshes which are injected into the body and eventually find their way into the brain where they unravel and spread out to sit on top of the neurons where they can "eavesdrop" and pick up the electric signals generated by moving neurons. The activity picked up by the neural lace could be connected to a computer to analyse the neural pathways in much the same manner as that seen before with implants. When tested in mice, the laces were accepted by the body in just five weeks with no noticeable side effects or rejections. The neural activity of these mice was then recorded for a further 8 months with limited observable health impacts. Not much has been heard from this technology since, suggesting it is a slow experimental technology in its early stages, but expect to hear more from this technology in the not too distant future.

Amongst the successful results of the neural lace experiment on rats was the observation that not only was the foreign material accepted into the brain without any adverse reactions, there were also indications that the mesh was actually merging independently with the healthy neurological matter of the brain. The significance here is the confirmation of earlier observations that the brain shows remarkable signs of cortical plasticity, i.e. the brain's remarkable ability to reorganize itself by forming new neural connections based on individual experiences, lifestyle, and environment. This suggests that BCIs do not have to be perfect thanks to the brain's impressive adaptability. Similar to how the brain has proven incredibly competent at picking up new tasks quickly (we can learn the complex mechanism of riding a bike within a few hours), the brain also learns new activities linked to BCIs in just as quick of a fashion. Researchers have noted the impressive learning times when connecting brains to robotic limbs; the brain starts to use the limb as a natural extension of the body very quickly and as accurately as the robotic components allow. It will be a relief to researchers knowing that the complex and delicate science surrounding BCIs will be made that much easier by a helping hand from nature. They are likely going to need all the help they can get.

Brain to Internet Connections

Head in the Clouds

Another thrilling possibility is a synergistic network between the brain, internet, and cloud. Long gone will be the days of manually typing queries into a search engine on that antiquated device once called a computer or smartphone. Simply subvocalize the thoughts in your head and an AI assisted BCI will induce the result of the query into your brain, either visually in the form of pictures and videos or through sound. Whereas we currently have the whole internet at the touch of a fingertip through smartphones, this information may one day be delivered straight into the brain via BCIs. Any information can be downloaded and, more notably, experienced. Language barriers need not be a problem any longer. An AI assistive BCI could work much like cochlear implants work today; an external microphone sensor picks up the incoming sound and sends it to the internet connected BCI processor. Once converted, the implant sends the processed sound signals to the cochlea where the hearing nerve fibres pick up the signals and send them to the brain as interpreted language.

Neural connections with the internet and cloud can essentially create non-synthetic memories. Any information you would ever need could be stored on the cloud or downloaded straight from the internet for future use, freeing up some of the finite but quicker natural memory. Medical students will be elated to not have to memorize the technical names for an endless list of Latin names just to pass an exam, instead, these names could be artificially "remembered" by simply downloading the pre-saved or searched information from the cloud. Eliminating fairly useless endeavours, such as remembering Latin names just for exams, will free up medical student's mental capacities for more practical exercises such as more mock surgeries where practice makes perfect, essentially creating more efficient and productive people.

Inducing Memories

A Trip Down Memory Lane

Further to downloading information and synthetic memories, it may also one day be possible to download experiences. Experiences are highly complex chemical and neural systems that are vital for human survival; a baby will learn to associate the sound and sight of its mother with pleasant hormones to indicate a position of safety. Conversely, a hedgehog will correlate getting harassed by predators as unpleasant and hormones will again signal to the brain that it is in a dangerous position and to curl up in a defensive ball. Every time the hedgehog encounters a dangerous situation the curl defence mechanism will be stronger and faster to ensure evolutionary survival.

How memories are actually stored is still not completely understood but is thought to be the result of bursts of neural electrical activity and how/when they are fired. After an event or experience that the brain deems worth storing (due to strong positive hormones such as the birth of a child or strong negative hormones such as getting attacked) the brain consolidates the events and the corresponding memories are stored throughout the brain as groups of neurons that can be fired in the same manner at a later date to recreate the event that caused the neurons to be stored in the first place (this process of storage and later recall creates what we know as a memory). Interestingly, the groups of neurons are stored in areas of the brain where it was created, e.g. visual memories from watching a film will be stored in the visual cortex and memories of hearing your parents read to you will be stored in the auditory cortex. Using the term "stored" is perhaps a bit of a misnomer; memories are not stored like a book on a shelf ready for recollection at any point, rather, they are collections of the neural firings created from the experience itself located all over the brain and then retrieved and encoded (pieced together). Researchers now believe that being forgetful if not as simple as the memory not storing (every brain process creates neural firings that are stored somewhere) but an issue with the recall/retrieval process. Therefore, a full memory is the piecing together of individual components of the memory, such as the visual aspect from the visual cortex, the sound aspect from the auditory cortex and the emotional component stored as neurons in the amygdala. The stronger the connections between these neural pathways, the stronger and quicker the resulting action. A boxer can, for example, punch much faster than an untrained person due to the thousands of repetitions performed during training, strengthening the neural pathways and the brain's ability to link the brain with the corresponding physical action.

To succinctly summarise, a memory is really the reactivation of neural connections between different parts of the brain caused by previous experiences. By understanding that the seemingly magic and intangible concept of memory is in fact based on a simple (in theory) series of neural firings between different parts of the brain, it may in fact be possible to recreate these neural firings through electromagnetic signal inducing techniques such as TMS (as we successfully saw earlier when experimented on rats and humans), in effect inducing memories into a brain which hasn't naturally and physically experienced the event/experience before. In theory, an inducer of some kind needs to induce electrical signals into the brain which stimulates and fires the same neurons that would have fired from the occurrence of the natural experience. This would "fool" the brain into thinking it has experienced this induced memory in much the same way as the natural experience would. Imagine having the neural pathways for riding a bike induced into your brain having had no prior experience in ever riding a bike. Successful riding involves using specific muscles in a rapid and coordinated fashion to balance the bicycle. This usually takes hours of ingraining "muscle memory"; the ability to reproduce a particular movement without conscious thought acquired as a result of frequent repetition of relevant movements. These hours of ingraining neural pathways could be artificially created by stimulating the necessary neural pathways from an external source.

All this, however, requires some way of knowing what neural pathways need to be created and the corresponding electrical signals needed to be induced. This would be far too complex for a human to do; there are a staggering 100 trillion pathways in the human brain and finding the correct combination for complex activities such as riding a bicycle would be logistically quixotic. With enough computing power, however, sophisticated and specialized AI algorithms could collect masses of information through many human samples. EEG scans of subjects carrying out specific tasks could be collected and analysed by AI to form patterns of neural pathways which we would then aim to replicate. The amount of data required to obtain these collections of neural pathways would be tremendous, however, and new storage technology would be needed to store, analyse and interpret this data. The technology will most likely be there one day, however, so this form of inducing memories certainly looks like a tangible possibility that could soon be explored commercially.

The potential possibilities with this technology are both numerous and thought-provoking. Thoughts, experiences, and memories could be shared between brains. Instead of sharing experiences of holidays through verbal stories and photographs, as is customary, mental experiences could be shared through the external stimulation of the neural pathways which created the experience. Live streams of your favourite pop stars, astronauts in space or even a family member away on business could be stimulated into your brain for a virtual recreation of the subject's experience. Once again, EEG scans of the neural pathways activated when recalling a memory (or when the experience actually occurs) could be identified, collected and stored for later induction into another brain.

Understandably there are sceptics aplenty regarding memory induction. Not only is the technology years away, we simply don't have a good enough understanding of the immeasurably complex mechanisms of the brain and its neural pathways. There is also the concern of misuse; the ability to delve deep into minds could be misused by those with heinous intent.

Synthetic Telepathy

A Meeting of Minds

No, you didn't just misread. And yes, in a book which promised to avoid attention-grabbing titles and misleading themes there is a section on telepathy. There is, however, a legitimate scientific justification for a form of telepathy which arises from the ability to both read and induce electrical signals into the brain using the same methods, such as EEG and TMS, seen previously.

Synthetic telepathy describes the process in which human thought (in the form of electromagnetic radiation) is intercepted, processed (through a brain-computer interface) with a return signal generated that can be processed by the human brain. The concept of synthetic or artificial telepathy hinges on the collection and interpretation of neural signals which are released from the brain before speech is vocalised. The determining factor on whether this ambitious field is feasible rests on the ability to generalize and interpret the signals and reliably translate the meaning behind them. If this proves viable, a mental lexicon of brain activity could be gathered and induced into a different brain using techniques such as TMS. Once sophisticated AI systems are introduced and tailored to maximise this technique the potential results would be hugely influential.

Perhaps unsurprisingly, the U.S. military and DARPA (The Defence Advanced Research Projects Agency) have backed the majority of funding as warfare and defence are two areas where the ability to both "read" minds and influence others is of boundless value. Being able to read and write to the internal monologue would allow for two-way communication for field agents without vocalisation, proving especially useful for situations where silence is vital. In the practical world, however, it is difficult to see how much more useful this would be over regular radio communications. Being able to "write" to the brain in addition to just "reading" could be of much more significance, however. Interrogations and intelligence gathering spring immediately to mind. Synthetic telepathy should be distinguished from mind reading insofar as synthetic telepathy merely records and interprets the change in electrical currents in the brain. We, therefore, cannot simply plug ourselves into the brain and force our way in, rather the subject must be thinking of the action we intend to read. The subject, therefore, needs to voice their thoughts and memories internally. This is possible when the subject and the reader have the same intention. In interrogation situations, however, a certain amount of psychological manipulation is needed to trick them into this mental talkative state, making the technology not much more reliable than a standard lie detection test.

There is also a concern of authoritative suppression. The body is simply the physical extension of the brain; the CNS receives impulses from the brain which in turn moves the targeted muscles. We have already seen the success from connecting bionic limbs to the CNS; the implants are able to code the neural impulses and translate them into mechanical movements of bionic motors. It is also possible to do the reverse. Feedback from bionic limbs can fire neural signals back into the brain for a sense of touch and force feedback. By inducing signals through TMS or other techniques, therefore, it could be possible to control someone else's actions through diminished mental control. Although an obvious public outrage would obviously halt this sort of practice in democratic nations, oppressive authoritarian nations such as China and Venezuela would be much more palpable. Since the flurry of tragic and embarrassing public protests in China after the events of Tiananmen Square, and the 1999 demonstration by 10,000 Falun Gong practitioners at Zhongnanhai, China has fiercely clamped down on any form of protest or dissent in order to ensure there is no opposition to the ruling communist party. The party now even restricts public gatherings of three or more people without official written permission from the ruling party. Synthetic telepathy technologies in the hands of these paranoid and oppressive nations will quite clearly further diminish the power and freedom of the people and could be used for crowd control or dissent suppression. Impulses could be generated and induced into the crowd resulting in a dispersion of crowds or a willingness to cooperate with authorities and to be used as a political tool. Once again, to be clear, this is not hypnosis but psychological manipulation without the knowledge of the affected person.

This may sound like balderdash but there have already been a concerning number of attempts to utilise this technology. An ITV news brief ("High-tech Psychological Warfare Arrives in the Middle East") in 1991 reported an attempt by US Psychological Operations (PsyOps) to induce feelings of fear and confusion in Iraqi troops in Kuwait. Due to battlefield complications, Iraqi troops were forced to use commercial FM stations to give and receive battle commands. This gave US troops an unprecedented opportunity to trial this new subliminal carrier technology called the Silent Sound Spread Spectrum (SSSS) by broadcasting to unsuspecting Iraqi troops using the 100MHz FM frequency. SSSS uses the studied brainwave patterns when a human experiences emotions and, after reproducing these patterns, places them on the silent sound carrier frequencies to trigger the same emotion in the targeted individual. This sort of technology is obviously very difficult to obtain any tangible results from, but even if it were, the controversial nature of this technology would ensure it remained under the radar as any acknowledgment of such a silent and deadly weapon would be political suicide.

We also know the former Soviet Union has dabbled in this technology. During the 1970s the Soviet KGB developed an eerily named Psychotronic Influence System (PIS) that aimed to manipulate the soldier's mental state and turn them into human weapons. The US defence agency DARPA has also patented numerous related innovations and has dedicated masses of funding to the field. Even if the technology is not obtainable in the near future, the value seen by various militaries certainly warrants prudent caution.

Despite the science behind the technology being incredibly fantastical, it could surface to be one of the deadliest weapons facing humanity today. Nuclear weapons are at least restrained thanks to mutually assured destruction. Silent weapons that leave no trace, however, provide a less risky attempt at espionage and the fact that they would be so difficult to prove in a court of law will tempt errant organisations. The human skull has no natural firewall against such intrusive weapons which are well suited to the cruel actions of mental torture and information theft. Whether such a weapon will ever be realised, let alone deployed, is at present impossible to tell, but the apparent legitimacy of the science behind the technology, and the power it would afford will be irresistible to all.

RFID Chips

With You Wherever You Go

We have already seen how implants linked directly to the brain are transforming not only how people function but also addressing the old age wonder of how the brain actually works. But implants are not limited to just the brain. Other implants are on the way and look set to change the ways we interact with both technology and each other.

RFID (Radio Frequency Identification) has recently been making steady progress in its use and application. RFID chips are tiny two-way radio communication devices roughly the size of a grain of rice and are inserted under the skin (usually in the web of skin between the thumb and forefinger) in a manner no more different than getting a piercing. The chip can provide various bits of information from personal ID numbers and passports to medical information and will continue to grow in its application as entrepreneurs and businesses find new and innovative commercial applications for them. Although the mere thought of inserting an electrical implant into the body will immediately put many people off, the thought of never needing (and never losing) keys and wallets again is certainly enough for me to be first in line.

Since receiving FDA approval in 2004, many volunteers have embarked on this micro-chipping adventure for a variety of conveniences. Wisconsin based technology firm Three Square Market has made available to volunteering employees an RFID chip installed by Swedish microchip leader Biohax. A surprising 50 out of 80 employees can now pay for food in the cafeteria and enter the building using nothing but a mere wave of the hand. Although the trial was most likely a fun publicity stunt of little current practical value and somewhat of a gimmick, the experiment shows the genuine public appetite for such a system and, for the many who are interested, the conveniences afforded outweigh the unnerving implantation.

The chips could also be very useful, and perhaps crucial, to medical teams in the event of an emergency. A simple scan of the chip could provide

medics with all necessary medical information, such as age, blood type, aller-
gies, and medical conditions. Such fast access to critical information would
undoubtedly provide quicker and safer treatments, potentially even lowering
health insurance costs. The technology could then gain traction quickly as
nothing peps consumers up as effectively as a hit to the wallet. If the technology were ever to become sophisticated enough to track and monitor live
statistics such as blood sugar levels, oxygen levels and other predictive pieces
of information, some incidents such as heart attacks and strokes may even be
preventable if enough of a warning were available.

Mass adoption by the public may make significant progress with the
ability to use RFID chips for convenient payment and access. I can't begin
to explain the eternal fury experienced trying to find my car keys in one of
many pockets, seemingly trying to summon the rains through a special spiritu-
al dance. The locks of cars, houses, work lockers and pretty much any lockable
device could be programmed to unlock via a unique code generated through
a personal RFID implant. Access can be granted and denied to anyone via an
app. Running out of cash or losing a credit card will never be an issue, payment
can be made by a simple hand movement.

Contrary to many new technologies which need a new and expensive
supporting infrastructure, RFID technology is already commonplace in today's
society. Animal and product tracking, inventory monitoring, passports, IDs
and driver's licenses all already contain chips which are read by RFID. Minimal
changes in infrastructure would be required to adapt; many train/bus stations
and airports already have RFID equipment in place.

Other novel uses of the technology are quite controversial. Weapon
manufacturers, such as Smith and Wesson and Browning, have already experimented with implant systems for firearms that allow only the programmed
owner to fire the weapon. Sensors on the firearm will unlock the safety mechanism only when the RFID implant of the registered owner is in range. Going
further, connecting all weapons with the IoT (internet of things) may even
mean every bullet could be traced through data such as GPS tracking and heart
rate of the user determining who discharged the weapon, where and when.
Police officers in the field would breathe a sigh of relief knowing that, if the sit-

uation turned sour, their weapon and vehicles could not be used against them. America, in particular, should be taking a special interest in RFID firearm technology due to its constitutional love of guns. Despite having just 4.4% of the world's population, America accounts for almost half of all civilian-owned guns in the world. This liberal approach to the right to bear arms means easier access to deadly weapons to those who aren't responsible enough to own them. As a result, there have been more than 1600 mass shootings since Sandy Hook and, on average, around one mass shooting each day. America, however, does not have more crime in general than any other Western Industrial nation; it just appears to just have more violent gun crime. With the NRA (National Rifle Association) contributing $30m to Donald Trump's presidential campaign, he is extremely unlikely to introduce any sort of weapons ban (his exact words were: "You came through for me and now I'm coming through for you"). But with increasing public anger, and unrest regarding the number and severity of recent attacks, Trump is being uncomfortably pressured by both public and business interests to take some meaningful steps in reducing these horrific events.

This is where innovations such as RFID chips could be a step in the right direction. Although current owners are unlikely to have an implant specifically for just a gun, chipped phones, bracelets and watches could be used initially until RFID implants are more commonplace for universal applications.

Whether or not RFID implants will be used for extreme applications like this remains to be seen; the variety and depth of issues where this technology can bring about positive change is vast and certainly worth discussing. Medical and housing data, in general, are amongst the most valuable of all data, presumably due to the high potential for advertisers to make sales. Implants which track medical data are therefore going to pay handsomely for any such available data. RFID implants cannot currently track data intensive streams such as GPS due to power and size issues (batteries and power storage technologies are currently not small enough to fit inside such chips) but once this technical hurdle is overcome (perhaps inductive charging or progression in micro-batteries), sensitive information such as location needs to be carefully and considerately regulated to ensure that the often powerless consumers are not exploited.

For better or worse RFID and other implanted technologies are coming and have the potential to change life for the better. From small conveniences such as digital wallets and IDs, they would allow for a much smoother and more synergistic interaction with technology. The potential for data and privacy intrusion is high, however, and although unlikely to ever become mandatory, like credit cards they could reach a point where not having one only serves to hinder (no credit history often makes it difficult to obtain loans). I for one am excited. Although a small step it is most likely to be the first on man's journey to become less man.

Chapter Summary

The time is drawing ever closer where the evolution of man may no longer be dictated by nature. Since the first successful sequencing of the human genome in 2003, it has been possible to identify every gene in a genome. The cost has dropped exponentially from $3bn to a nearer $1000 and is expected to soon cost less than $100, making it possible for almost everybody to have access to a detailed blueprint of their individual genome. With this knowledge comes great power, and the ability to modifying these genes is progressing quickly. The evolution of the human race will soon be in our own hands; we have the responsibility of not only exploring this technology but also ensuring it is used fairly and safely for all.

Illnesses and diseases that have long scourged the planet may one day be a thing of the past. Haemophilia, HIV, and cancer may one day be tackled much more efficiently at the source, if not completely eliminated. CRISPR is the most promising of current techniques and, upon identification of the defective gene in question, can locate, cut, destroy and replace defective genes, solving the problem at the most fundamental level. Despite being conveniently simple to programme, the off-target mutations from previous trials clearly denote the infancy of the technology and how much is currently not known about the potential side-effects. The severity of the side-effects will delay the commercialisation of this technology; only when results reach very near the 100% mark will these forms of gene therapies be allowed.

Whereas gene therapy helps only the individual who is the recipient of such procedures, the results die with that person too. Germline modification, however, focuses on those genes with are heritable and can be passed down upon reproducing. Although the potential benefits are great (complete resistance to viruses could be achieved), so too are the risks. The genome is so vast and complex that off-target mutations, which have been so prevalent in testing, could go unnoticed and passed down through generations. The dangers here are enormous, they might not even be released for decades, in which time irreversible damage could have been caused. There are also ethical concerns regarding eugenics and the ability to modify genes which are not therapeutic but merely for reasons of self-interest. If rules and regulations allowed, genetic modification for non-therapeutic purposes would certainly be available when privately funded; the demand for genetic modifications such as height and eye colour would be tremendous. It would, however, only be available to those who could afford it, perhaps creating a cycle of improvement for only the elite minority who can afford it. Those who cannot would potentially be at an immediate disadvantage in almost all aspects of life. Again, government rules and regulations need to keep pace with development to ensure that the use of such therapies is fair and equal.

Aside from genes, BCIs are also primed to alter the capabilities of the natural body. Whilst most bionics and BCIs have currently focused on the noble cause of restoring human functions back to their normal capabilities, it won't be long before they start to delve deeper and take the human body beyond its natural limits. The ability to not only read but also write to the brain opens avenues for extremely disruptive applications. Memories and experiences could be manually induced. Mind to internet and mind to mind connections could become the norm. The uses of this technology are limitless, but the possible misuse could result in disastrous consequences when in the wrong hands. The ability to safeguard the brain against possible misuse needs to be a top priority and needs to keep pace with the rate of change. The mind is the most delicate of human assets; to be deprived of mental freedom is the worst torture of all.

8. Employment

Will You Make the Cut?

Congratulations on making it to the final chapter. You are now equipped with an overviewing knowledge of some of the most innovative and disruptive technologies we can expect to see in the future, some much closer than others but all close enough for society, and you, to start preparing for. You may be feeling a plethora of feelings from being overwhelmed and concerned to excitement and enthusiasm. But what you may now be wondering is where you, as a skilled or unskilled labourer, employer, business owner, engineer or even student about to embark upon a future career path fit into the picture and what will become of you and your profession in the years to come. For some, there will be opportunities to seize and innovations to benefit from. For others, there will be redundancy and difficulty ahead. One thing is certain, however; the need to educate yourself to be best placed to make decisions that could affect not only your career but your life, your children's life, and even your children's children's life. Below is an objective overview of the impact future technologies could have on employment.

An Overview

A Blast from the Past

When attempting to plan for the future, the best tool is often looking into the past. The industrial revolution of 1760 - 1840 is often cited as the first major economic adjustment period resulting from the introduction of new technologies. During this transformative era, new manufacturing process-es, a transition from hand production to machines, the introduction of new chemical and iron production processes, the increasing use of steam power and the rise of the factory system raised Britain's manufacturing prowess and made it a major technologically advanced country. Initially, the consequences of the transition were mixed; although wages increased alongside productivity, child labour became a sadly common occurrence due to their unique ability to fit into small machine openings and the lack of rights they were afforded by society. Work in these mechanised factories was also excruciatingly hot, long and, as anyone who has worked in a factory in a pre-health and safety era can attest, repetitive, unsafe and exhausting. Working conditions gradually improved thanks to government regulation and compassionate industrialists, an act which needs to be remembered as we move into a new digital revolution.

The overall impact on the majority of society and the economy was positive, however. Introductions of technologies such as steam power and industrial machinery increased the productivity of individual employees and business as a whole, leading to increased wages and an increase in new jobs necessary to operate and tend to these new machines. Increased wages also had the secondary effect of increasing consumer demand as people now had more disposable income to spend on luxuries such as better and more nutritious food and leisure activities. This, in turn, increased demand for products and services, which spurred business growth whilst creating further jobs, thus continuing the cycle of prosperity. Transport infrastructure also improved alongside the need to distribute these new products and people, further boosting trade. The larger distribution networks increased the demand from businesses, opening new opportunities such as bigger textile mills which needed more employees to meet demand.

With the power of hindsight, it is now clear that mechanisation and automation of the industrial revolution did not lead to widespread suffering or major social upheaval as we fear of today's revolution. Instead, factory productivity improvements increased both wages and the total number of jobs, spurring consumer demand for more products and services, further increasing the supply for this demand and continuing the cycle. The growth that transpired in the following couple of centuries was unprecedented and has undoubtedly improved the quality of life experienced today. The steam revolution of this period is known as the first of four revolutions, with the second being the introduction of electric power, enabling mass production techniques. The third saw the mass use of electronics and information technology to automate production whilst the fourth sees the blurring of borders between physical and digital realms as we are currently experiencing today.

Productivity vs. Employment

Sleeping on the Job

You would be forgiven for expecting a similar economic pattern to that experienced during the first two revolutions; productivity improvements increase wages and employment, creating more disposable income, spurring more consumer demand and, in turn, starting an iterative cycle of self-improvement. Whilst for most of the second half of the century, the US saw the economic value generate a rise in line with employment; this trend now seems to be diverging. After the devastating effects of the financial crises, much of the developing world has been enjoying periods of record low unemployment. At the time of writing (2018) the UK has an unemployment rate of just 4.1%, a 40 year low, and the US has a similar story at 3.9%, the lowest rate this century. This, however, has not corresponded in an increase in productivity, the main indication of increasing prosperity. This is concerning in an age of computers, smartphones and all manner of new and productive innovations and technology, and has many economists and business owners worrying about the future of employment. Is there cause for concern?

Firstly, it is important to note the difficulty of accurately defining the root causes of the weak productivity experienced since 2000. There are many theories, some more positive than others. The statistical analysis techniques used to analyse productivity data have come under scrutiny as of late. Whereas manufacturing output from physical products, like manufacturing, is relatively easy to measure as it was during the industrial revolutions, measuring service sectors such as finance and the aerospace industry are much more difficult. More developed and richer countries tend to deviate away from manufacturing (outsourcing to less developed countries is cheaper) into service based trading which can return better profits thanks to the increasing ease of doing business globally. The UK, once a leader in manufacturing output, now has an 80% service sector based economy. It is therefore thought that outdated and inadequate measuring techniques are not fully capturing the effects of service-based economies. A second more bleak theory reckons that earlier waves of innovation in technology (computers, outsourcing functions etc.) have fully saturated the economy and are no longer adding any further effect to it. This is further exacerbated by a lack of business investment as a result of austerity measures employed after the financial crisis, as well as cheap loans raising the debt levels of companies in a period of increasing interest rates and high corporation tax.

Optimists, however, suggest that low productivity is the result of an early investment in technology and human capital that is yet to pay off, much like how new businesses typically do not see a return on investment until years 2, 3 or 4 of operation. The low employment statistics suggests businesses have invested greatly in human capital, which will one day pay off and increase productivity as a whole. Whatever the reason, automation and robotics are thought to be involved to some degree.

Technological Unemployment

The Optimists

One of the most notable and revered economists of the 20th century, John Maynard Keynes, was the first to popularise the theory that causes many sleepless nights for economists the world over. Technological unemployment defines the loss of jobs caused by technological change. Such change includes the introduction of "mechanical muscle" such as robotics in vehicle assembly plants and "mechanical minds" such as software and algorithms that can utilize bucket loads of information to make (hopefully) more accurate predictions. But whereas Keynes stated it was "only a period of maladjustment", are the negative consequences from the upcoming technological revolution avoidable? Is the wave of transformation too powerful to prepare for as software reaches and exceeds some areas of human capability?

That technological change can cause short-term unemployment is both obvious and accepted. Self-service checkouts as are commonplace in supermarkets today and clearly replace a person on the tills. Whether this technological unemployment leads to longer-term unemployment, however, is controversial. The pessimists' voice has become louder as the correlation between productivity and employment has deviated from historical norms, seeming proof that the two are now not as related as was once thought. If productivity no longer relies on employment (and hence people) then will people be displaced by machines that better improve productivity? It is clear that if machines and automation increase bottom line profit companies wouldn't think twice about adopting them. This pessimistic approach, however, fails to recognise the secondary effects of automation, what economists call compensation effects.

There are five main compensation effects that are thought to create prosperity from innovative technologies. The first is the need for human labour to build these automated robots. ABB is a leading technological and automation company that provides "innovating digitally connected and enabled industrial equipment and systems". Operating in over 100 countries, the company alone employs over 132,000 people, the majority of which wouldn't have had an industry to go into had automation never occurred.

The second compensation event is the resulting new investments occurring from higher profits realised from the cost savings of automation. A company usually does one of three things with profits: buy back shares, return to shareholders through a dividend or invest it. Investing in new staff, new areas or new products will more than likely result in more jobs for its new business activities.

A third effect is the change in wages. At times of high unemployment, such as through an envisioned period of technological unemployment, wages will decrease as workers fight for jobs. Lower wages are more attractive for employers who can now perhaps afford to employ 1200 workers when wages are $10 an hour compared to just 1000 at $12 an hour.

The fourth effect is lower consumer prices resulting from lower costs of manufacturing goods. Efficient automation can eliminate the majority of labour (labour is usually a significant cost in manufacturing) and hence bring the cost of appliances down.

This, in turn, results in the fifth and final compensation effect, the demand for more products. Lower product and consumer costs allow disposal incomes to stretch further, increasing consumer demand. There will be a corresponding increase in supply to match this demand whose innovation will directly create more jobs.

These compensation effects apply to society as a whole and are thought to be the reasons for the economic prosperity following the industrial revolutions. These effects are also compounded by what is known as the job multiplier: the amount of direct, indirect and induced jobs created (or lost) in an area. According to research by Enrico Moretti, an American Economist, for each additional skilled job created in high tech industries such as AI and robotics in a given city, more than two jobs are created in associating non-tradable (service) sectors. Additional research from Europe shows local high-tech jobs could create up to five low-tech jobs.

The Pessimists

And the Winner is...

During previous technological revolutions the pessimists towards technological unemployment have been few and far between and, in hindsight, the optimists proved to be correct. The consensus in the 20th century among professional economists and the general public remained with the view that technology does not affect long-term unemployment, with only a couple of notable exceptions in the 30's and 50's (these bursts were quelled by the build-up to war). This belief also held true for the first decade of the 21st century. Since 2010 however, attitudes have shifted significantly as technology has advanced much more rapidly than many predicted and rising employment has not resulted in a corresponding increase in productivity.

Both pessimistic and optimistic economists now agree that compensation events did indeed result in economic prosperity and its associated job growth. The pessimists (who are growing in numbers) now argue that the returns from compensation effects are significantly diminishing due to the capabilities of computerisation. While automating machines of the 19th and 20th centuries increased the efficiencies of hard labour, they were unintelligent and needed large armies of human operators to remain productive. Computerisation, on the other hand, often does away with human interference altogether.

Another important difference in today's technological unemployment is the unequal distribution of job losses. Machines most often perform "easy" work such as assembling cars. The task is simple, routine and usually performed by unskilled workers with few qualifications. It is these poorer, less qualified people who are out of work whilst more jobs open for more qualified people. This qualification gap increases as technology become more capable and the "easy" jobs may now include those which were deemed more difficult and white collar. The remaining "hard" will soon require higher levels of intelligence and mental capacity than the majority can provide, forcing the less capable and less intelligent majority out of employment. The fourth digital revolution we face today is likely to provide economic prosperity and job creation, but mostly for those with the mental capacity, intelligence and qualifications to fill these more intellectually demanding jobs. The most obvious solution is to re-educate and retool those who are set to be displaced by automation, which should be implemented through government programs and initiatives. Even experienced and talented professionals such as MBA business leaders are taking online courses and degrees to ensure their abilities and knowledge remains up to date and that they remain competitive in rapidly changing environments.

Hopefully, you are now equipped with a contextual outlook of the effect on the economy with the advancement of technology and automation. Whilst history suggests that automation increases both productivity and employment, the recent deviation between these two figures suggests this trend may no longer hold true. Some sectors will struggle at the expense of newer, more innovative industries. Let's take a look at the potential winners and losers so you can better place yourself as an individual in this larger picture.

Winners and Losers

Winner takes it all

With increasing integration of robotics and AI systems into the workplace, it is no wonder there is such an outcry over machines taking jobs from man. A 2014 Pew Research report found a split opinion from 1896 technology professionals and economists regarding the effects from automation. 48% of respondents believed technology would displace more jobs than it would create by 2025. Another 2016 report by the United Nations estimated that 75% of jobs in the developing world were at risk (loose term) from automation, with developed countries affected more than developing countries due to the more dominant service sectors. Although concerning for those affected, it should come as no surprise. Businesses will always look to boost profits and cutting costs while increasing efficiency is a major part of that. One European bank has asked Indian outsourcing company, Infosys, to cut staff numbers in the operations department from 50,000 to just 500.

A common view is that automation in the labour market mostly hurts those with low skills (cleaners, fast food workers, construction labourers). These jobs are seen as repetitive and easy to replicate, two areas where robots excel. The 2016 Economic Report to the President estimates that 83% of jobs with an hourly wage below $20 were at risk from automation as well as 31% of those between $20 and $40, and just 4% of those above $40. This operates on the premise that higher paying jobs are associated with higher skilled labour or management services which are more difficult to replicate. There is also evidence that automation is now responsible for suppressing wages. A 2018 Brookings Institute study analysed 29 industries in 18 OECD countries to find that, despite automation slightly raising the total number of jobs available, from the 1970s to the 2010s it contributed to a slowing of wage growth due to increasing productivity from robots decreasing the value added to work from human labour.

As technology becomes more sophisticated and capable, concerns are spreading beyond low skilled at risk jobs to intermediate and even high skilled jobs. White collar jobs are also now at risk as repetitive computer tasks such as data analysis and middle management are becoming increasingly automated. More recent studies, such as the 2016 Economic Report to the President, have looked more at wages than the skill class of labour. Oxford academics Carl Benedict Frey and Michael Osbourne have predicted that in the half of all the jobs expected to be made redundant, a strong correlation between income and education and the ability to be automated was found, including not just labour but also office-based computer jobs.

All these studies must be taken with a pinch of salt; although the general trends may be somewhat accurate it is unwise and unreasonable to instill fear amongst all low skilled workers. Many low/medium skilled jobs are unlikely to be automated, such as emergency plumbers, as the unpredictability of the work makes it extremely difficult to replicate. A better way to categorise at-risk jobs is by the nature of the work and how easy the fundamental skills of work are to replicate.

Repetitive/systematic Tasks

The first, and most obvious, nature of work likely to be automated is repetitive and systematic work. Systematic work such as factory and assembly line labour where the work is "easy" and replicable is, and has been, the first to be automated, with Henry Ford's assembly line pioneering this transition over 100 years ago. Repetitive work, which usually accompanies systematic work, is also the most at risk to be automated as robots and computers can be tailor-made for specific jobs and can, therefore, perform these repetitive jobs faster and cheaper than human labour. Humans understandably get bored and distracted doing this sort of labour, so, assuming those who are displaced can find alternative work, eliminating these sorts of jobs is a win-win; companies benefit from increased efficiency and productivity and workers no longer have to be subjected to monotonous work.

Such repetitive at-risk work includes translation, legal research and even low-level journalism (fact gathering). Fast food sector workers are at particular risk as they face an inevitable battle between minimum wage and automation. As the minimum wage and cost of automating technology continue to converge the likelihood of replacing workers with robots grows. There will be a point where it is more cost effective to replace human labour with machines. In September 2016, nearly a quarter of all restaurant closures in San Francisco Bay cited increasing labour costs as a reason for shutting down, according to Forbes.

Restaurants have already responded by introducing self-ordering kiosks which are now commonplace. American fast food restaurant, Wendy's, installed 1000 of these Kiosks in 2017 to combat rising labour costs and slowing growth. McDonald's has also followed suit. After announcing in June 2017 the installation of self-service Kiosks in over 2500 restaurants, McDonald's shares hit an all-time high, highlighting investor sentiment towards the efficiencies of automation and opening the gate for others to follow. McDonald's are now pushing for smartphone ordering, ironically replacing these new robotic kiosks with mobile phones. Even the machines are getting replaced by more modern machines.

Office jobs, often thought to be safe from the rise of the robots, are also at risk. Tasks such as managing finances and paying suppliers are easily replicable and actually benefit from being automated (no late payments as people can forget). This also builds corporate trust knowing the company you are doing business with has an unbiased and reliable payment system in place as well as making routine backoffice work more efficient.

Data Intensive Tasks

The second category most at risk from automation (and already suffering) is those jobs which require fast and accurate collection, analysis and interpretation of data. The advancements in processing and storage capabilities of computers has enabled more information to be collected, proving immensely profitable for companies and advertisers. The advancement in software has also contributed to this data revolution, increasing not only the scale of data collection but also the depth (deeper information, such as medical history, is more valuable to advertisers). Data collection and usage are areas which prove highly advantageous to computer's very specific processing and storage capabilities, two areas which have seen computers exceed human capability very quickly and by many orders of magnitude.

For some, this has resulted in direct job losses. Financial data analysts have seen a major reduction in the number of available jobs as algorithms are able to use AI systems to obtain data from various input sources and interpret them into spreadsheets of numbers and ratios with no bias, and with the benefit of large sample sizes, to present directly to managers who can act upon them. Junior lawyers are also on the firing line as AI algorithms are able to search through hundreds of thousands of documents from large databases much more quickly and accurately than a human can.

While the minority will be completely replaced by data automation, the majority should benefit handsomely by working alongside such systems. Doctors are perhaps the most immediate beneficiaries. Doctors are well known for spending half of their time in front of computer screens researching information and looking through patient records. An increasing amount of these data-intensive tasks will become delegated out to software systems, most likely to the benefit of already stretched medical staff and their employing institutions.

Researchers at the John Radcliffe Hospital in Oxford, England, have developed an AI heart disease diagnostics system which has already proved more accurate than doctors 80% of the time. This is not to say doctors are poor at diagnosing heart disease, it is merely an example of how powerful AI systems can be when given enough input data. Harvard University researchers have also found similar results with a "smart" microscope that can detect potentially lethal blood infections. The AI system draws results from a large sample of 100,000 images of slides treated with dye to make the bacteria more visible with an impressive accuracy rate of 95%. Perhaps the best demonstration of the power of AI data systems comes from IBM's Watson general purpose algorithm. When man and machine were pitted against each other for the task of gathering meaningful insights from genetic data of tumour cells, what took human experts 160 hours took IBM Watson a mere 10 minutes. Examples like these are abundant and increasing in both application and accuracy by the week. They show how perfectly suited computers and their software can be when dealing with large data sample sizes and the ability to draw meaningful correlations from it.

Whilst these algorithms have the power to perform data-intensive functions much more quickly and accurately than their human counterparts, we should not fear their disruptive potential. Whilst some are at risk of losing out to these machines, the vast majority will benefit from utilising them for personal gain. The productivity and efficiency gains realised from AI will free up more time for doctors to actually engage with their patients and administer treatments. Many welfare institutions, such as the UK's NHS, are already stretched, resulting in lengthy waiting times and ultimately poorer customer service. Instead of reducing medical jobs, AI will reduce waiting times for patients to the great benefit of all involved. Doctors can finally breathe a sigh of relief.

Interpersonal Skills

This is another main category of skill which, certainly for the foreseeable future, should be safe from automation. In fact, jobs which depend upon forms of tacit knowledge (knowledge which is understood without having to actively learn) such as creativity, social intelligence, teamwork, leadership, listening, dealing with people and managing crises and conflict, are set to prosper. These skills are collectively understood to be "know how" skills rather than "know what" skills and are currently extremely difficult to replicate.

Advertising and promotions managers display high levels of both creativity and emotional intelligence, targeting their ads, not just to the strength of the product, but to how well they can create an emotional link with their target audience. Architecture is another similar area; a computer would most likely design buildings to optimise the engineering efficiency. An architect, however, engages in a never-ending battle with the designing engineer regarding aesthetics vs. buildability. Knowing what aesthetically pleases humans is completely tacit; the Mini Cooper car was designed to look curvy to mimic the inherent human appreciation for curvy women (which biologically suggests fertile, and hence healthy, mating partners). Recreating this with a computer would be immensely difficult.

Those who deal with the human mind are also in a strong position. Mental health and social workers use very high levels of tacit skills, from listening and sympathy to problem-solving, whilst also identifying when and where the best time to use each of these skills is.

In general, mid to high-level managers who are responsible, to some degree, for the drive and direction of a company are most likely to not only hold on to their job but to also prosper. These traits cannot currently be mimicked but are responsible for the significant growth of businesses. One cannot usually shift from a factory floor to middle management, however; these jobs require a certain level of intelligence and mental capacity that not everyone possesses.

Man and Machine

One of Us

The recurrent theme thus far has not been the mass elimination of jobs as "experts" have been fear-mongering for the last decade or so, but rather a new era of productivity where man utilises and maximises the advantages computers and robotics can offer in pursuit of increased productivity. As opposed to competing against technology, we will be competing against others with technology. Markets and industries are likely to become very competitive as business efficiencies and productivity tightens, leaving less slack and room for error in the system. Amazon shows an early insight into how this may look. Over the last three years, the company has increased the number of robots working in its warehouses from 1,400 to over 45,000. Yet over the same period, the rate at which it hires new staff hasn't shown any signs of slowing. The reasoning behind this is the same as we have seen throughout this chapter; robots increase productivity, minimising costs for consumers, consumers buy more resulting in an increased demand and hence the need for more employees to match this demand.

The robots Amazon employ do not, for the most part, replace workers, rather they replace parts of the jobs to which they can exceed human limitations, such as fetching products from warehouse shelving. It is thought that very few of these jobs can actually be fully automated, but most will benefit by having machines automate parts of the process and freeing up their human counterparts for activities in which they are more productive. This idea of a man-machine synergy is important to remember, for these jobs are likely to become both more numerous and higher paying in the future.

Elon Musk is currently experiencing the difficulties of completely automating manufacturing processes first hand at his Tesla car production plant. The serial entrepreneur has had his shareholders on the edge of their seats as his Model 3 car production facility has consistently failed to hit production numbers due to an overreliance on AI and automation, tweeting "humans are underrated". Other jobs face similar problems. Postal delivery firms may well have fully autonomous fleets in the future, but they will not be able to walk up stairs or access gated properties.

It is expected that the vast majority of employees will see a gradual increase in software tools at their disposal, delegating the repetitive and data-intensive tasks to machines to free up time for humans to do what they do best; using their creative and interpersonal skills. It is important to emphasise the gradual aspect; automation will not be a tidal wave of revolution displacing every one of inferior capability. The expensive, time consuming and, in some cases, controversial aspects of introducing technology into the workplace will ensure that change remains well-paced, giving those who need to retool or readjust time to assess and alter their career paths. The partial automation of jobs where employees have more time to do a smaller amount of tasks will not necessarily eliminate the number of jobs either. It is more likely that freed time from these partially automated jobs will be used to perform other functions where humans can add more value. Where factory workers have part of the build automated, for example, they may now take on quality control tasks to ensure the components created by robots are up to a satisfactory quality.

Preparing for the Future

Easing the Blow

We have now heard both the pessimistic and optimistic points of view for the future prospects of jobs and employment; the optimists look to the past and observations that productivity boosting machines spur economic activity and hence job creation while the pessimists maintain that the effects of computerisation reduces significantly the need for human interference and weakens the compensation effects that drove prosperity after previous revolutions. While the unity between man and machine is set to increase worker productivity (much like Microsoft Word and Excel have done for office staff), whether this trend continues indefinitely is less likely. The plethora of research and studies can only estimate future trends with today's knowledge i.e. the technology we have available to us today. Who knows what the future holds and whether tacit traits such as creativity and interpersonal communication will one day be replicable. Although generally unforeseeable today, neural networks and more powerful AI may help us learn more about the brain, how it works, and how it can more easily be mimicked. With such a hazy view of the future beyond 20-30 years, therefore, it would be sensible to adopt one of the prevailing suggestions of this book; to prepare for the worst. A world economy where humans are unable to work would be catastrophic for society. Fortunately, researchers, entrepreneurs, businessmen, and governments are already exploring options for an era of mass redundancy.

Universal Basic Income

Money for Nothing?

Although job security, on the whole, looks set to remain not only safe but prosperous in the near future, there may well come a time in the mid to long-term future where machines advance to such a degree where it causes employment levels to drop to disruptive levels. This disruption would have a massive negative impact on the global economy and would cause painful damage to an already declining middle class. Less employment would severely reduce income tax streams for governments, in turn reducing government investment in local services and infrastructure and ultimately ending in a cycle of reduced spending, austerity and a decline in living quality for all.

There have been several ideas devised to ease the pain of such a scenario, some more practical than others. If automation decreased labour demands but also increased productivity and wages, we could simply adopt this sort of culture through reduced working hours. In 1870 the average American worker averaged about 75 hours per week, dropping significantly to 45 prior to the start of WWII. Thanks to increased productivity and wages, however, the reduction in working hours still resulted in similar household incomes. The reduction in working hours worked well as worker productivity increased to match the reduction in hours and overall output remained the same. People were happy to reduce working numbers during the war as people were willing to share the work to keep as many people earning as possible as well as to enjoy their new found time off for the increase in leisure activities resulting from an increase in national productivity. This trend could continue, perhaps resulting in a four-day work week. As long as the reduction in working hours does not result in a corresponding decrease in overall output, overall consumption will not decrease and the economy will continue to flow. One might even argue that more free time would result in more consumer spending and hence an increase in economic growth.

Bill Gates has taken a more audacious approach through a devised "robot tax". The robots which replace human workers would be taxed at similar rates to what their corresponding human counterparts would, in theory maintaining government income tax revenue streams. This would not only slow adoption of machines over humans but would also avoid (to some extent) profits from machine labour lining corporate pockets and help to evenly distribute the wealth from mass use of efficient robots. Whether it is fair to place the financial burdens from technological change on businesses is questionable, but it may be necessary; consumers with no money to spend (and therefore no demand) will hurt business in the long run and negatively impact the whole economy.

A more practical theory for maintaining consumer spending during periods of mass unemployment is the universal basic income (UBI). This would take the form of a new kind of welfare regime in which all citizens of a country receive a regular and unconditional sum of money for which a basic but livable income would be guaranteed. There would be no pressure or requirement to work, perhaps creating an understandable public outrage toward a lazy and unproductive society. The main reasoning behind this theory is to firstly ensure those displaced by robots do not fall into a state of poverty while also ensuring consumer spending does not drop to low enough levels whereby the economy would suffer. In its purest form, a UBI would be totally independent of income, meaning both the poorest and wealthiest would receive the same periodic income.

Several countries are either planning for or currently actively experimenting with different forms of UBI systems. Switzerland rejected such an idea in a 2016 basic income national referendum with 77% of voters rejecting the proposal. Other countries have had more success. In 2017 Finland undertook a pilot program where 2000 citizens each received a monthly income of €560 ($640). Despite hopes for an extension after the initial two-year trial, the government has decided to halt the program to pursue other, presumably more promising opportunities. Kenya is also in the early stages of a smaller scale trial with results expected to be posted in the near future, whilst other countries such as Scotland are also in the planning phases of trialling. The largest current trial is in Ontario, Canada, where 4000 participants have just been enrolled. The many trials which are either in progress or in the planning and enrolment phases are yet to post any results, but governments and economists the world over will be eagerly awaiting the results of this ambitious theory.

Despite good intentions, the universal basic income suffers from a couple of major flaws that will most likely prevent it from ever being realized. The first of these is the sheer cost to implement. A study by the Institute for Policy Research (IPR) at the University of Bath estimates the total cost to the UK at £288bn per year, equivalent to 9.4% of GDP. This figure pitches UBI at the current rate of existing benefits (£72 per week for working-age adults with payments higher or lower for children and pensioners respectively). To make this cost revenue neutral, i.e. cost the state the same as the current means tested system does now, all major wage replacement benefits such as state pensions, child benefit and the elimination of income tax personal allowances and lower National Insurance bands will need to be abolished and replaced with this single UBI monthly payment. An increase in income tax of 4% would still be needed to match today's levels of spending. It would also have unacceptable distributional consequences; many working adults will now face higher rates of tax with minorities such as the disabled, who need higher levels of welfare support, worse off. There appears to be a triangle of compromise in which the three parameters of success (controlling costs, meeting needs and maintaining work incentives) cannot all be met at the same time; there has to be a compromise. There is also a broader compromise between UBI in general and the current means-tested welfare system. The incumbent system ensures a more favourable compromise between meeting the financial needs of beneficiaries and controlling costs but at the expense of administrative complexity and adverse work incentives. UBI, on the other hand, avoids most of these problems at the expense of controlling costs. As with most compromises in business and politics, it usually costs which dominate decisions.

Negative Income Tax (NIT)

Turning a Negative into a Positive

Although UBI's flaws may prove too significant to be deployed on a large scale, the underlying idea of supporting lower earners should not be abandoned altogether. A negative income tax (NIT) could support lower earners while minimising the cost to the state and providing a better incentive to work.

NIT takes the form of a progressive income tax system where people who earn below a predetermined income level receive supplemental pay from the government. While those above the threshold continue to pay tax to the state, those below will not be taxed but will see income given to them to meet the minimum income needed to live sustainably, hence the term negative income tax. UBI gives money unconditionally to all, meaning earners over the threshold will have to return a proportion of that income back to the state in the form of income tax, creating inefficiencies through double-handling money. NIT, on the other hand, only allocates money to those who earn below the threshold. An NIT would create a single welfare system that fulfils the social goal of an adequate standard of living for all (such as with UBI) that could be sustainably funded through taxes. This also helps to reduce "welfare traps" as is common with incumbent welfare systems, such as minimum wage workers whose net income is actually less than when unemployed because of the removal of welfare once employed. No matter the income, the higher the earnings the better off you are, theoretically eliminating issues with work incentives. An example best clarifies how such a system would work. If the tax exemption level is $20,000 and income tax rate is 50% (subsidy rate is equal to income tax rate) then someone earns nothing would be given a 50% subsidy for the difference they earn below the exemption level (50% of $20,000 = $10,000). Similarly, earnings of $10,000 would receive a $5,000 top-up (50% of $10,000 difference) and earnings of $15,000 would result in a $2,500 top-up (50% of $5,000). Earnings of $20,000 would receive no subsidy whilst also paying no tax. Someone earning $30,000 would pay $5,000 tax and a high earner of $100,000 would pay $40,000 tax. The more is earned the more tax is paid, theoretically funding the subsidies for lower incomes from those with higher incomes. Whether this is fair is debatable, but the chances of politicians being brave enough to agitate their biggest source of funding and backing (the wealthy) would be slim. Reworking the very complex and entrenched nature of most countries tax laws would also be a burdensome and disruptive task. But the system is at least theoretically viable.

Although the incumbent means-testing methods are not likely to disappear anytime soon, it would certainly be a worthy task to at least address the feasibility of these welfare systems as a backup plan in case automation does one day create mass employment and its inevitable economic doom. Even if the ideas prove impractical we can at least move on to the next idea. The economic fate of the world is on the line after all.

Education

Learn the Hard Way

Successfully navigating society's way through future decades depends on equipping the next generation with the necessary skills to thrive in an era of high technological requirements. As we have seen, the rise of technology usually brings with it a net gain in job creation through secondary compensation events. The difference this time, however, is the nature of these new jobs. They have changed from labour intensive (maintenance of steam machines etc.) to highly analytical and intellectually demanding (software and robotic developers). These high-level jobs are usually protected by qualifications such as degrees and won't be open to the low skilled workers who are most at risk without significant retraining. These degrees are also expensive and time demanding, two factors which do not help the average working man where he sells most of his waking time to provide for his family.

This new digital revolution has the potential to significantly increase productivity and economic growth, benefiting all who participate. The opportunity, however, will be constricted significantly by a lack of comparable growth in the education system. An outdated and unfit for purpose education system is now not capable of producing the correct skills in enough quantity to meet future needs, hence the significant shortfall in software engineers, developers, mechanical engineers and IT data analysts.

One does not have to go back to school or university to retrain, however. University degrees are becoming both more expensive and less prestigious. University rates have increased from 2% in 1945 to over 43% today (England, 2018). The larger degree base has naturally diluted its value. Degrees still dominate, however, not necessarily due to the educational value and the content learned but because employers still demand them; they link a degree with intelligence, commitment and other values that set their candidates apart from the rest of the employment base. Often a name from a prestigious university such as Yale or Harvard is much more valuable than the actual content learned. This is why MOOCs (massive open online courses) haven't lived up to their expected potential. These online courses were expected to disrupt universities in much the same way as digital media companies such as Facebook and Spotify have disrupted the news and music industries. MOOCs have not taken off as expected due to the high weighting employers place on a certificate from a respected institution.

Recognising this, incumbent institutions are now setting up their courses online. Arizona State, Berkeley, and Yale have all created online degree courses offering the same level of education and professional recognition for a fraction of the price. The average US cost of a degree is $85,000 compared to $30,000 for online courses. Online courses also forgo the burdensome costs of living away such as rent, beer, and late night pizzas. There are some drawbacks to online courses; learning will be more difficult when studying alone and it takes a lot of self-motivation to study when raising a family or working. Employers also tend to look down slightly at online degrees as opposed to traditional ones but as they become more popular, online degrees from respected institutions already established with traditional campuses are becoming ever more tolerated. Online only universities with no campus presence will usually be held in less regard, something to remember when applying for online courses.

The average online student is employed and in their mid 30's. 56% are married, 50% had at least one child and 78% were employed. Most of these working students have 12 years or more experience and are taking online courses to meet and get ahead of future demands and colleagues in rapidly developing sectors such as business administration, nursing, computer science, and engineering.

Although degrees will always be an important component in job seeking, it may not be enough to keep pace with future demands. The severe shortage in specialist occupations such as software development and business management may see employers hire based on metric testing of the candidate at an individual level. Thanks to the advent of sophisticated AI and data processing systems, individual traits such as memory, attitude and risk can be tested, helping employers identify how the candidate would suit the role in question. Companies such as Unilever, a consumer goods company, and Nielsen Holdings, a global information, data, and measurement company, recruit candidates from AI tests which gather information in some 80 traits which the company deems preferential for the hiring role. In theory, this not only helps those candidates without degree qualifications but helps recruit candidates which are better suited naturally for specific roles. By having a larger talent pool to hire from (as opposed to just those with degrees) employment and skills gaps can be avoided, helping boost productivity. Ideally, testing would also be unbiased, helping reduce the minority employment gaps and create a fairer working society. I can see this sort of metric testing becoming a lot more popular over the years once companies start seeing productivity improvements from staff.

Whilst the rise of online degrees and training would be of great use to those individuals seeking to either retrain or boost their position in rapidly changing environments, this alone will not be enough to meet future demands for skilled employees in new innovative digital fields. For this, education needs to be evaluated at a national level, starting firstly in changes to schools at primary and secondary levels. On its current trajectory, the incumbent education system will not meet future demands especially in the science, engineering, technology and maths subjects (collectively known as STEM).

The first concern is the limited access to education faced by many developing countries. The lack of ubiquitous education stifles innovations and slows global growth and productivity. Niger has one of the worst education rates with the mean number of years at school a mere 1.5. Barely 15% of the nation can read and write and 31% drop out in primary school. For girls, it is even worse. The children in question have the same potential as anyone else; the potential is being lost to circumstance, however. Who knows how many potential Nigerien Albert Einstein's or Charles Darwin's have passed us by. This potential needs to be unlocked and ubiquitous access to education is the cornerstone.

The major barrier to ubiquitous access to education lies in the inability to find and pay teachers who form the backbone of a strong educational system. Technology can provide ways to reduce the impact of this burden such as remote learning using a pre-set curriculum of online videos and tutorials. This is not ideal; good teachers are priceless when it comes to teaching not just content but social and behavioural skills that can only be transferred through direct communication. Although school syllabuses are important, it is arguably the tacit traits such as communication, creativity and social interaction that are just as, if not more, important in an era of automation. In areas where good teachers are scarce, however, online content could be a cost-effective and efficient alternative option to a basic quality of teaching.

A second concern is the nature of the content taught in classes itself. The formulaic approach that has remained dominant for much of the past century has served children well to date, but times are changing and the content is failing to keep up with changing economic demands. Traditional exams at secondary and university level are largely dependent on memory. Doctors have to learn a plethora of Latin names just as engineers are forced to learn the constants and properties of materials. In an age of instant access to most information, this use of large mental capacity is both unnecessary and inefficient. Much how learner drivers in countries such as the UK must now learn to navigate via satnav, schools should reduce the focus on memory tasks and teach how to efficiently and effectively utilise access to vast amounts of information in order to keep up with the times. Closed book exams currently limited by memory should be replaced with active solution seeking problems where the candidate has access to as much information as they would in the practical working world. This would arguably provide a better test of intelligence, problem solving and creativity; traits which have been identified by many as essential to prospering in a digital age.

The age of boring PowerPoint presentations and 100 student lectures should be replaced with more interactive and perhaps technology-driven solutions. Instead of trying to explain the complex and hard to visualize nature of shear forces and bending moments in steel beams through words and numbers (as my painful civil engineering memory recollects), active computer renders with dynamic responses to loading, which are much easier to grasp, should be used. Essentially technology should be utilised to better reinforce academic principles where it best assists our understanding, such as visual representations of difficult concepts.

This is not breaking news, however. Governments the world over have identified the need to update modern educational procedures, but once again it all boils down to funding. In austere times funding is simply unobtainable. Between America's renewed conflict with Russia and their political meddling, North Korea and its nuclear weapon program and China expanding its military presence in the South China Sea, defence budgets are at a recent high. Little funding is left available for education at a time when it needs it the most. Some US state funds have dropped so low that schools can only afford to open 4 days a week. Many teachers are on measly pay starting around $32,000 and are being forced to move across borders to seek better teaching jobs, intensifying problems for those underfunded states.

Business can step in where governments are failing, however. They certainly have the incentive to intervene; research suggests that for every $1 invested in a child's education $53 is returned to the company in productivity gains. In the Global Corporate Sustainability Report of 2013, education was identified as a top priority for the private sector to address. Of 1000 CEOs asked, almost 30% identified a lack of talent as a reason for not pursuing market opportunities, and in countries of the Association of Southeast Asian Nations, this rises to over 50%. Yet despite the reward, the private sector contributes just less than 0.1% according to a UNESCO policy paper from a sample of some of the world's biggest companies. Private investment in developing countries' education is higher, although still only 5% of all aid. Other issues such as AIDs and malaria bring a much larger investment, possibly due to the immediate gratification and results which make it easier to warrant their donations. The results from education investment, however, are long-term and are much harder to quantify, meaning less support from shareholders who need to justify spending in the short term. Education forms the basis of all aid, however; educating about AIDs and malaria could stop infection in the first place as opposed to reactively treating it. For every year a young girl is in school they are much less likely to become pregnant and more likely to obtain a sufficient salary. Whilst aid for malaria and AIDs is certainly a worthwhile and noble cause, they are fairly reactive i.e. treating the symptoms of a problem. Education, on the other hand, is more proactive and allows for prevention of the disease altogether, resulting in a much more efficient use of resources.

Whether the severe shortage of talent in business is enough to drive investment in education alone is unlikely; business executives are often limited by the whims of their short-sighted profit-seeking shareholders. Governments could provide quotas or tax incentives for educational investment. Better would be a cooperative between business philanthropic business leaders for an educational investment fund. Powerful individuals have the power to instigate great change too. Bill Gates has used his wealth and influence to make a massive impact towards global healthcare. Another figure of this stature could encourage the private sector to invest in its future performance and champion the cause for good universal education.

Chapter Summary

Past experience from three technological revolutions has provided us with quantitative proof that, although there will be some short-term issues, innovation results in increased productivity, higher wages, job creation and therefore economic prosperity at both an individual and national level. This historical norm, however, is now becoming less prevalent as productivity and employment are starting to diverge. Despite some of the highest levels of employment seen for decades, productivity and wage growth are stagnating. The fact that output is not growing despite an increase in labour suggests humans are adding less value to businesses than they were previously. A dissociation of humans from productivity encourages businesses to look to cheaper and more efficient machines and robotics to compensate.

The exact reasons for this divergence are not precisely understood. While some blame the statistical modelling techniques as being insufficient in an era where services dominate, optimists suggest that investment in technology and human capital is yet to pay off, while pessimists argue that hard economic times, cheap debt and a lack of investment are suppressing innovation.

There is a strong correlation between pay and the ability of a job to be automated. Lower paid jobs tend to be lower-skilled and are mostly "easy", systematic and repetitive tasks where machines can be specifically engineered to perform them quicker and cheaper. As robotics and AI systems become more capable, higher skilled and higher paying jobs will become progressively more at risk. These are just trends, however, and are mostly inconclusive; some low skilled jobs such as emergency plumbers or builders cannot be automated and will continue to prosper. Similarly, some skilled labour which falls into the above categories is increasingly becoming automated.

Tacit traits inherent to human behaviour will become increasingly important in job security and wages in an era of disruptive technology. There will be a higher demand for creativity, communication, and interpersonal skills with the rise of new innovative companies vying to push their products/services.

Of the jobs economic prosperity could bring, a high proportion will be highly skilled and intellectually demanding, such as software engineers and managers. A large number of the workforce will not have the intellectual capability to perform these demanding skills, potentially resulting in both a shortfall in talent and a glut of employable low skilled workers.

Automation itself, however, is not as likely as many believe to completely automate whole jobs away. Machines and AI algorithms have the potential to automate some repetitive or data-intensive aspects of some jobs, such as analytical data work for doctors. This allows for better job focus on tasks which provide better time value and require human skills, such as doctors spending more time interacting with patients. The benefits from automation come from utilising it to make people more productive in their roles.

Just because mass technological unemployment is unlikely to happen anytime soon doesn't mean society shouldn't be prepared for such an event. A universal basic income could pay an unconditional sum of money to all, regardless of the situation, to which a basic economic quality of life could be achieved. Despite a recent increase in support and trials, the triangle of conflict between costs, meeting needs and an incentive to work may always ensure it stays in the realms of theory. An extension of the theory, the negative income tax, could provide a better incentive to work whilst not emptying the government coffers, and this form of taxation may become more prevalent in upcoming years. What is certain, however, is the need to reform educational systems to ensure the rapidly changing needs of the future workforce are met and a lack of talent, as is already becoming evident, doesn't stymie the potential economic and social benefits of innovation.

As for you personally, I refer you to a comment made by Google's chief economist Hal Varian: "Seek to become an indispensable complement to something that's cheap and plentiful". We should not seek to compete with machines for that will be a losing battle. Those who learn to work with and leverage the advantages machines provide will be the biggest winners.

9. Conclusion

We initially set out to identify and evaluate some of the most disruptive and influential technologies and developments in the immediate few decades. We also wanted to see how these innovations will affect you, as a blue or white collar worker, business owner or student, whilst also identifying the need to leverage these technologies to ensure your higher productivity places you at the top of the competitive tree, allowing you to advance where other less prepared and less productive people will struggle.

AI will become an area that will permeate into almost every workplace in the near future. The complexity and rapid evolution of the subject, however, makes it very easy to get lost in. Companies will look to increasingly more efficient and capable AI systems to increase business productivity where human labour is starting to fail. Repetitive, systematic and data-intensive jobs, such as call centres, data analysts and customer service reps, will see their job largely replaced. Finding similar work will also become increasingly more difficult. These AI systems, however, will always need some form of manager or interpreter to turn the results into action. Those who have an understanding or qualification in such systems will be infinitely more likely to move up than those who don't. Again, those who fight and fail to adapt will lose out to those who have prepared and embraced change.

In terms of the future of AI itself, artificial intelligence may not be so artificial forever. Approaching the topic in terms of physical atoms and molecules, human consciousness and the trillions of neurons and connections, which has long thought to be a non-physical trait only associated with humans, may one day be replicable. In absence of the evolutionary and biological limits imposed upon humans by nature, an essentially limitless digital brain could be capable of a much higher level of intelligence, demoting humans to the second most intelligent being on earth. What a situation like this would mean for humans is currently inconceivable, but one cannot help but feel great apprehension. It is vital for regulation to keep such a technological singularity from overwhelming our ability to control it.

IoT connected devices and cloud computing will change how we interact with technology. Smartphones and wearable tech will become deeply embedded into our lives, perhaps too much. Our phones will be used to access our homes, cars, and workplaces while watches and implants will continually monitor our bodies and alert us to abnormalities long before any physical symptoms reveal themselves. Our reliance on it, however, may become one of our biggest weaknesses. A connection failure in an "always on" hyper-connected world would cause significant disruption to a fast-moving society.

Autonomous vehicles will also drive great change, particularly in city centres where pollution and congestion are quickly reaching damaging levels, both environmentally and economically. This will force local and state governments to ban the use of polluting vehicles and charge for road use based on how, when and by who they are used. Congestion and high costs of ownership are already taking their toll on the incumbent car ownership model, with many young working urbanites ditching their personal car in favour of ride hailing and sharing. Once autonomous, the total price per mile for car hailing and sharing will drop to levels below that of traditional car ownership, rendering the use of a private vehicle impractical to all but the wealthiest. The current system of free road use will have to change to a pricing policy, such as a price per mile, to ensure road infrastructure keeps up with demand. With the advent of smart technology and the IoT, tracking and charging vehicles will become much easier and ubiquitous.

Powering this new wave of electric vehicles, and other such energy demanding technology will require a major change to an already stretched electricity network. Fossil fuels will not be able to meet future electricity demands and the environmental damage is already approaching irreversible levels. Renewable power is becoming more common as prices for solar panels have decreased but their use will remain mostly circumstantial. The varying climate for many geographic locations results in intermittent power generation that limits the amount of renewable energy that can be reliably depended upon. Instead, they will have to be combined with other dispatchable sources to smooth out variances. Initially, incumbent sources such as gas and coal should be relied upon where the plants are already built, with coal plants phased out after the lifespans of these existing plants expire. Cleaner natural gas will take its place until a more efficient source of dispatchable proves feasible. Nuclear power is looking to be the most viable candidate for this role. Once the initially high, but notable falling, costs of building nuclear plants matches that of natural gas, the larger power generation capabilities and lower emissions inherent to nuclear should see it finally break free of its precarious image to become the dominant form of energy production.

Technology will soon advance to such a point where the boundary between man and machine will be indistinguishable. Genetic modification, bionics, and brain-computer interfaces will take human capabilities beyond what it took nature 200,000 years to achieve. Techniques such as CRISPR will allow for targeted isolation and modification of specific genes, initially for medicinal purposes such as the targeted removal of HIV, cancer and haemophilia defects, but later expanding to more trivial ones. Height, strength, eye colour and intelligence may one day be programmable into genomes, but only to those who can afford such privileges. The possibility of a genetic divide subject to nothing but circumstance will ensure the topic remains controversial for some time.

All these discussed topics will play their part in changing the nature of many jobs. Advancement of such technology has lessened the value of human labour on productivity, fuelling legitimate concerns that an era of mass redundancy and automation is on the horizon. Even if this were proved true for the majority, it does not have to be the case for you. It is true that those jobs which are systematic, repetitive and data-intensive will become increasingly vulnerable to partial or full automation. But where opportunities close, others open. Managers who can use their interpersonal, creativity and problem-solving skills will find themselves in a very advantageous position. Boost your resume by taking online courses and prove to potential employers that you are better placed than the rest of the competition to embrace this new wave in technology. Technology can make their human counterparts more productive; can you imagine how long financial documents would take without the use of excel spreadsheets? Learning is earning; as long as you are increasing your knowledge and experience base, you are moving in the right direction. This brings us back nicely to our original premise; fighting and resisting the inevitable change in technology is a losing battle and will bring nothing but pain and misery. You can prolong it as long as possible but this will only prove to delay the inevitable whilst also prolonging the pain. Fortunately, the opportunities are so plentiful you don't need to. Those who learn to work with the flow of momentum will be better placed to leverage it to their benefit. By embracing and learning from the change, you will be much better placed to grasp its opportunities. No quote sums up the lessons from this book better than that from the Roman philosopher Seneca. "Luck is what happens when preparation meets opportunity". By preparing for a changing future, as we have seen in this book, any opportunities that will come your way can be better seized upon, ensuring you do not get dragged down by the tides of change but sail with them to a land of opportunity.

www.ingramcontent.com/pod-product-compliance
Lightning Source LLC
Chambersburg PA
CBHW030934060726
47591CB00005B/1799